APR   6 2009

W9-BZY-202

PSYCHOLOGICAL NUDITY

Savage Radio Stories

PSYCHOLOGICAL NUDITY
Savage Radio Stories

FIRST EDITION
FIRST PRINTING

MICHAEL SAVAGE

SPI
SAVAGE
PRODUCTIONS INC.

www.michaelsavage.com

First Edition, First Printing, October 2008

Published in Las Vegas, Nevada by Savage Productions, Inc.
P.O. Box 27740, Las Vegas, NV 89126.

ISBN Number 978-1-4276-3401-6

Any or all persons represented herein may or may not be completely fictional. Anyone reading this book who thinks they may recognize one of these characters should immediately seek psychiatric help.

Printed in the United States of America

08 09 10 11 12   5 4 3 2

For Janet, Becky and Russell
who have traveled
this long and difficult road with me;
without whom I would not have made it.

CONTENTS

CONTENTS

CONTENTS

CONTENTS

Introduction

Each day is an adventure into the unknown. There are many "stories" in everyday occurrences: every day brings the opportunity for joy, compassion, redemption.

By listening, we can learn to hear again.

By observing, we can learn to see again.

By conversing, we can learn to speak again.

Only by turning *off* the media-fed stories can we hear our own story, and by shutting off the stream of images we can see what is real. By speaking and listening, even in the market, we can, again, capture our own voice.

The "stories" in this volume were selected because they stand out from my years of telling what happened in my everyday life. Did I leave anything out? Sure. Could I write another 10 volumes? See Laurence Sterne's novel, *The Life and Opinions of Tristram Shandy, Gentleman,* where mere sidesteps became the show.

I end my book with a storm surrounding me, "the autism storm." The enemies of freedom want to write my autobiography, but I will not let them dictate the narrative of my life.

The style in this book can be seen as a distant ancestor of the first "storyteller in a cave" or the ancient Jewish prophets. Laurence Sterne later developed it as a literary form in *Tristram Shandy*, written in 1759. With these influences in mind, I have become known for my "stream of consciousness" radio stories, and this book captures some of these streams.

THE ELECTRIC BLUE
SADDLE-STITCHED PANTS

In the 7th grade, my mother bought me the most incredible pants. We didn't have a lot of money, but she knew I wanted these pants really bad. It was the "Elvis era." Mama Savage saved and bought me a pair of electric blue saddle-stitched pants. I wore them to school—I thought I was Elvis himself.

On the very first day, a bigger, older kid just happened to be wearing the same pants, and naturally, we got in a scuffle. He pushed me down and my gorgeous Elvis pants were ripped in the knee. I thought it was the end of the world because these were the most expensive, beautiful pants I had ever had in my life. So, the rest of the day I couldn't sit through the classes. Whatever the teacher said, my mind was somewhere else. My heart was pounding: *How am I going to tell my mother? How am I going to tell my mother?*

So, I came home with the pants, hiding the rip under my coat. I said, "Ma, I ripped my pants." She didn't get mad. She said, "Let me see them. Don't worry about it." I said, "You're not going to tell Dad, are you? She said, "No, don't worry about it." So all night long I couldn't sleep.

The next day the women were talking it over, sitting around the little table in that little house in Queens, and they were moving the crumbs around with their bread knives and talking. They decided what to do: they took the pants to a certain tailor, and the word came back: "Don't worry, Michael. The pants can be weaved."

Now, I didn't know what "the pants can be weaved" meant. I don't think they do that anymore because clothing has become something different than it was then. We throw everything away. But I knew from that moment on that everything would be good—and it was. The pants were weaved.

That's what a mother's for, I guess: to fix everything but a broken heart.

THE FLY IN THE TUNA:
Story of Savage's Father Standing Up for Him

"Dear Dr. Savage, please tell us when your father stood up for you," asked a caller. I'll tell you exactly. It was when I was a wee lad; that would be between the ages of eight or nine. Skinny, polo shirt, dungarees, spring or summer, Saturday, probably working with Dad in the little store down there on New York's Lower East Side.

He would send me for lunch out on the mean streets in order to toughen me up, because he thought I was too soft growing up in the suburbs. He insisted that I go walk alone in those horrible streets and learn how to fend for myself—dodging the garbage, the rats, the thugs, and whatever else was in the street. It was only dangerous up to a point. It's not as dangerous as some kids face today in the average housing project, but it was a bad neighborhood in those days—and certainly different than the Garden of Queens in New York where we were living.

So, he would send me for lunch. There was a dairy restaurant, where they had dairy only and no meat. They would serve tuna fish salads, whatever. It was filthy dirty. If you didn't want the meat from Katz's Delicatessen that was down the street, this place was a "no meat joint." So he sent me for a tuna sandwich. I came back with the tuna sandwich, and my father opened it up and there was a fly in it. He was enraged, so he took me by the hand. He was mad that they would give this kid, his son, a sandwich with a huge fly in the middle of it. He assumed they did it on purpose. They probably did; they were spiteful.

He took me by the hand, put down his work making lamps or whatever he was putting together for the day, dragged me up the street, with his neck bulging, veins bulging, eyes bulging. He went into the dairy restaurant and screamed at the guy, "How dare you give my son a sandwich with a fly in it!" The guy said, "Let me see the sandwich." He opens it and sees the fly in it. He says to my father, "I didn't charge him any extra. What are you yelling about? I didn't charge him for the fly." You know, it's an old joke, but it wasn't funny.

In a way Dad was standing up for me, I guess. I think that's the one time I could say "quasi" standing up for me, because, other than that, truthfully—I mean he even took our dog Tippy's side after the dog tore my leg open, now that I think about it. It was like an Abraham and Isaac relationship: I think if he had the rock and knife I wouldn't be here today. Thank God he didn't collect box cutters and there were no large rocks in the back yard. That's all I can say.

SYMPHONY SID STORY:
Growing Up in the Age of Radio

Here's a portion straight from one of my shows, talking about one of my favorite radio voices:

Play another song for me, because I'll sing a little and I will talk a little: that's all I'm going to do today. "Jumping with my boy, Mike, in 'The Nation.'" Let it roll. Oh, stop the music. Wait: I've got to hear this again. This is one of my favorite pieces of music. We had my guys dig it up. Hold it: This is Symphony Sid—the theme song of Symphony Sid, who was a great disc jockey in the 1950s. You've got to understand what I'm talking about: this guy was the night voice of America.

We had a lot of American jazz in NYC. You'd be coming home at 2 or 3 o'clock in the morning, whenever, and there was Symphony Sid with his gravelly smoker's Scotchy voice. And you were on the way home, and you knew the world was right. Tell me, who plays a saxophone like that today? Nobody! And he had a laugh on him. When this guy laughed, the world was OK—I don't care how bad your day was.

I'm very lucky: I grew up in the age of radio. I don't know if you know this. I don't want to talk about nostalgia—I'll sound like an old man, and I'm not. But I did grow up in the age of radio. There was someone who wrote an article recently who said that some of the great people in radio today grew up in the age of radio. I grew up on my father's knee listening to the radio.

To this day I can still smell the second-hand smoke I got from Dad's Phillip Morris. If what is true about second-hand smoke (which of course it isn't), I should have been dead at 11. I can still see his yellow nicotine-stained fingers and me dozing next to him, listening to "The Green Hornet." You had to use your mind listening to the radio plays back then. Today it's all spoon-fed; you don't have to use your mind anymore.

So, it's left to guys in the radio business to say it like it is. When I play Symphony Sid on my show, here's the memory chip: Silver Cup Bread Factory, over the 59th Street bridge, 3 o'clock in the morning, coming home from the Latin dance clubs; smoke coming out of the Silver Cup Bakery, going down the Long Island Expressway. Another 8 minutes to home: it was cold. It was late. Gotta be at school or work the next day. That's it—the whole piece.

4

TOUGH HIGH SCHOOL GEOMETRY TEACHER:
Two Fingers on His Right Hand

I had a geometry teacher in high school with only two fingers on his right hand. He was a tough guy. He was an Irishman and real tough, but a very good teacher—the kind of teacher who made you come up to the blackboard and perform. If you didn't, he ridiculed you. He didn't curse you out, but he called you a dummy. As you stood there sweating, he might say, "Now what's the matter with you today? Is your brain not functioning?"—that kind of thing. Believe me, you didn't want to wind up in front of that blackboard not knowing your stuff because you didn't want to be humiliated in front of your peers.

Today, of course, they take any moron off the street; any idiot who has one eye going up, one eye going down; who can hardly speak; and they tell you he's smarter than you are. If you dare be smarter than him, you go to the back of the class. But in those days, it was very clear: if you were smart, you were smart. If you were stupid, you were dumb, and that was the end of it. No one changed anything.

He had a left hand with five fingers and a right hand with two fingers. The two fingers were stubs, but he could still put chalk on the board. When he said to you, "The mid-term exams are back," he would read out every name and every score—publicly. Now, why do you think he did it? Because he understood that by doing well you were proud of yourself and the other kids looked up to you, and, by doing poorly you were ashamed of yourself, and you would try to do better. But now, because the liberal nuts took over the schools, where they try to put perversion ahead of everything else, they have now taken dummies and tried to make them better than the "smarties." Consequently, the schools can't even teach

Johnnie how to add or read—and if Johnnie isn't smart enough and he can't focus at all, they put him on Ritalin to dope him up and turn him into a sissy and a dumbbell who can't do anything except sit in a cubicle for the rest of his life and possibly jump off a building when he's 25.

Now, how Mr. W. lost his fingers is another interesting story. We all heard the rumors. It was whispered in the halls of the high school that he lost his fingers— and I'm not glorifying it—planting a bomb for the IRA. Now, I don't know whether it was true, but it was certainly enough to make us understand not to mess around with this teacher, and we didn't. We respected him. Whether it was true or not is irrelevant. That's whom we had for teachers in those days: many tough men, most of them vets from World War II.

HAPPY AND SAD CUFFLINKS

No question, if I was a kid in school today—let's say, in the sixth grade—they'd put me on every mind-controlling drug imaginable. The mean-faced, clipped-haired women would say, "That little Savage, he has shining eyes and he talks too much. Put him on Ritalin. Put him on Prozac. Put him in a straight-jacket. He shows all the classic signs of maleness. We must kill it. Kill it! Crush it!"

I believe most mothers don't even know what their poor boys go through in school. When I was a young boy, my mother bought me a pair of cufflinks. They were a set of the thespian masks—you know, one was a sad face and one was a happy face. I loved those cufflinks. I'd look at them when I was bored in class. On my right cuff I had the happy face; on the left sleeve I had the sad face. Some days I'd switch them around and put the happy face on the left sleeve and the sad face on the right sleeve.

Many days I was so bored I didn't know what to do. I'd look at these cufflinks for hours in the classroom while the teacher was going on and on about George Washington and the Delaware River. I was so bored I spaced out. I learned that George crossed the Delaware, he saved the country in Trenton, he overthrew the British—I got that the first week of kindergarten! They're still teaching it to me in the fourth grade. In the fifth grade, I learned what a peninsula is. In the sixth grade, it took them a year to teach me what an island was. I couldn't take it!

So, I stared at the cufflinks: the happy face, the sad face.

When I got bored with the cufflinks, I'd start pulling hair out of the skin on my arms. Today, they would have put me on Ritalin or put me in a nut house. They'd call my lack of attention a disease. It wasn't. It was called boredom! I inflicted pain on myself rather than listen to the teacher bore me one more second.

Rather than improve the curriculum, teachers today might say, "Oh, your son has something wrong with him, Mrs. Savage. We found out that he looks at cufflinks instead of listening to the teacher talk about how evil America is and why white males need to be put in the pillory. He's pulling hair out of his arm, and we suggest you put him on a moderate dose—just a moderate dose—of Ritalin on the first day." That's for starters. Soon, the teacher might say, "Let's put him on Prozac."

Now, I'd be the first to admit that teaching is a tough profession: keeping the lesson engaging day after day takes everything out of you. As long as I live, I'll never forget the day I first walked into a classroom to teach. Maybe I'll write a book about it one day. You know, something for the students. I could call it *The Savage Guide to Surviving Junior High School.*

Anyway, back then I didn't look much older than the students. I had graduated high school at 16, which means I in turn graduated college very young. Frankly, I decided to grow a goatee to look older than the junior high school kids in my class. I remember when I raised my foot to walk over the curb the first day, to step into that junior high school, and my foot froze up—I actually stopped mid-stride. The students were racing past me to get to class and I was standing there as stiff as a statue!

I had no idea I had a fear of teaching, but I did. If you think teaching is an easy job, try it someday. It is probably one of the toughest jobs on earth if you do it right. So, when I'm critical about the teaching profession and the teachers union, don't get me wrong: I fully recognize it's a tough drill. At the same time, there's no excuse for boring students to death. If an uneducated man like Woodchuck Bill could teach me about life then surely I should be able to do the same with my college degree—at least that was my view.

10

WOODCHUCK BILL

As a kid I loved the summer—what kid didn't?—because in those days you didn't go to summer school. You didn't go to a camp to advance your mathematical knowledge, another to advance your sports knowledge, another to lose your tubby waist. You went and had fun for the whole summer. Without the ball and chain of school holding us back, we were liberated. We'd come alive. Those were such wonderful days: those eight hot weeks when the sun didn't set until 9 p.m. At the first change of the seasons, somewhere around mid-August, I remember feeling the impending return of slavery. The first hint of fall was announced by the thunderstorms, and I'd feel the shackles of school coming back. I knew I would soon be returning to my horrible, mean school, in corduroy pants, armed only with a meatloaf sandwich. I'd have to face the teachers and chalk dust and bullies in the bathroom. It was awful.

When September rolled around, I was doomed.

Let's not make any mistake about it: personally, I hated school. I detested the testing. What do you think, that because I went all the way through the system and got two masters and a Ph.D. that I somehow loved it?—I never did! Learning is supposed to be a discipline, not "fun."

We were kind of poor, so what we did during summer was, to get out of the hot inner-city, the family rented a small cottage with all the other families from the neighborhood and relatives up in the cool Catskill Mountains. We stayed in what were known as bungalow colonies because you basically got one room—kitchen, bedroom, bathroom all in one room—and your whole family was in there. Then the whole "colony" was filled with your friends and their parents, so it became a little village. Naturally, it was paradise because every other parent was your parent and you reverted back to another time in history: we'd play Indians out in the woods and carve trees and make canoes out of birch bark.

In one of these bungalow colonies, there was a guy who was a caretaker who lived in an old abandoned barn with his wife. That was Woodchuck Bill to us kids—it was a Tom Sawyer experience. We loved Woodchuck Bill. Bill was unlike any teacher I ever had at school. Man, could he tell stories!

Now remember, he was not a bum. See, today they're a bum; they're homeless. He was what was known as a "hobo" in those days, and there were people who were hobos, who were sort of respectable in their own way. That was his job category: he'd put it on the IRS, like the "what do you do" job category. Hobo. I don't know what he made—next to nothing.

Woodchuck Bill would regale us kids with his stories. He was a big guy with a big stomach on him. I remember him saying, "Alright, kids, come over here." Today he'd probably get arrested just for even telling us a story. "Alright, I want all of you to punch me in the stomach." Now, right away that's rape today—it's raping a child in some way. So, we'd all go up with our skinny little arms—we were nine, eight, seven—and we'd punch him in the stomach, and nothing would happen. So, naturally, we thought he was Superman. He must have been pretty strong when you think about it.

Anyway, so we all hit him. We realized we were nothing compared to Woodchuck Bill. Then we'd sit at his feet and he'd tell us stories. He'd say— I remember to this day, he would say, "Well, I've seen hurricanes and I've seen tornadoes." We sat spellbound, like out of a book from the 19th century. What I liked most about Woodchuck Bill was that he lived in this barn with almost nothing. He had his few pots and pans, which hung from hooks. We'd say, "What do you eat?" And he said, "We eat woodchucks." Who knows if he was telling the truth—I don't know if you can eat a woodchuck.

Hanging around Woodchuck Bill is the perfect example of the education I got outside of school that was just as important to me, if not more so, than what I'd get in a stuffy classroom. As "odd" as Bill was, he had such insight into living and enjoying life and being an independent thinker. He possessed a pioneer spirit that made us think we could tackle the world with our bare hands. Woodchuck Bill is long gone now. I only wish kids today could experience the education I got from a man with his kind of streak of independence! Unfortunately, students are rarely introduced to men and women of courage, honor, inspiration, or other traditional principles. Instead, thanks to the Left-leaning teachers' association, the schoolhouse has become a hothouse of radical ideology. Instead of simulating students' minds, they're taught to stimulate other parts of their bodies, from kindergarten to graduation.

SAVAGE LIKED ART IN GRADE SCHOOL AND HUBRIS IN ADULTS

I'll never forget a prize I won in the third or fourth grade in the Bronx. In-between fending off the blows of the fellow students and having my lunch stolen and protecting my shoes and clothing, I actually learned something. One of the things we did was paint. That was a lot of fun. It was sort of a violent jail for young children, P.S. 48.

I remember getting into George Washington: it was the first picture I ever did. The teacher said, "Pick any topic you like," so I picked George Washington crossing the river at Trenton, at the front of his boat. I remember getting into the swirls of the water—I just got so into it, I lost myself, with the waves and the boat. When I finished the painting she said, "This is very good, young Savage." They made me go around the whole school with it. I was embarrassed. I was ashamed, because I was not yet in talk radio. Today, of course, what you do is take the smallest thing you do and make it into the biggest thing. Back then you took the biggest thing you did and it was always the smallest thing because you were a child without any hubris. But, as an adult, you need hubris to survive. Without it you're just a penniless, helpless worm.

FAT PAT & TIPPY THE DOG

When I was a boy, my parents moved us from our Bronx apartment to live in a small row house in Queens, New York. At that time, we got a dog named Tippy. Tippy the dog was a ferocious part-Chow who, when I was 11, ripped my foot open. I'm not talking a scratch here—he treated my foot like a lamb shank! I actually had to be hospitalized and get stitched up! I still loved Tippy the dog, even though the doctor was trying to get us to take him to the pound to be gassed.

Tippy was a male, which might explain his crazy temperament. The truth is I happen to prefer owning a male dog. Why? I don't know how to do this in a delicate manner—you know, every once in a while a female dog has a thing happen to her and it's a mess. And, no, I don't believe in having your dog "fixed." I didn't buy a pet just to spend all my time and money at a vet!

Now, aside from taking a bite out of me, the worst thing that Tippy ever did when he was little was to mess the house. Dog owners know that's what happens until they're trained—you get used to that. However, when a dog grows up and knows how to do its business outside, another problem surfaces. Once or twice a year, Tippy would go into heat. I remember how he'd jump on my father's friends' legs. Whoever came into our house, Tippy would try to mate.

This was a real problem because people were always coming to our house. They all knew my mom loved to cook, so day and night they'd drop in on us. True, it was a different day and age: people could just stop by for conversation. It wasn't like today, where you have an appointment a month in advance.

For us, just about every night someone would knock on the door. My mother would make coffee and they'd sit in the living room and talk for hours.

But when Tippy the dog was in heat, watch out.

One guy in particular drove Tippy insane. I don't know why Tippy focused on Fat Pat, but he did. Fat Pat must be dead 20 years now. This guy was like a character out of *The Sopranos*. You know, he had a size 25 neck. Rumor had it he was a bookie—Fat Pat always seemed to have something shady going on the side, if you know what I mean.

Still, we kids loved him. He was just a lovable, giant sort of guy, always laughing, always good for a joke. Don't ask me why, but Tippy especially loved him, too. When Tippy went into heat, if Fat Pat was sitting in the living room, Tippy the Dog would jump on Fat Pat's leg and grab it with his huge paws. The two of them would go crazy in the living room! Tippy would start rockin' and rollin' on Pat's leg; Pat would laugh and laugh, rolling his head back on the soft couch.

Picture a fat guy rolling back, laughing as the dog's humping his foot: the women are screaming. I'm busting up. My mother gets a broom and starts hitting the dog. She chases Tippy with that broom like a Samurai warrior. She'd yell, "Get out of here! What are you, an animal?" We'd lock Tippy up in the basement. He'd be barking and making noises like he was King Kong down there. Everyone else would go back to the coffee and cake.

There's a lesson here: unlike humans, my dog went into heat, once a year or whatever. But human males, especially those in college, think they're in heat every night. They've been brainwashed since kindergarten into thinking they're supposed to be in heat 24/7, and then they wonder why they're impotent half the time!

But, going back to Fat Pat. He worked in a seedy hotel as a "nightclerk" but he was really a pimp. Now you immediately think he's a bad guy, right? Listen to this before you jump to conclusions. He and his wife could not have children. One day Pat brought home a little girl from his "hotel". A little girl who was the product of one night's lust with one of the girls from the hotel. He and his wife raised that little girl as though she was their own! But wait, it gets better.

Years later Fat Pat brought home another child, this time an infant boy, from Hotel Lust. His wife's sister raised that child as if he was her own! Years later, after Pat died, that adopted girl took care of her "mother" right up until her last day. Do you think today's soul-deprived world would see a pimp bringing home a love-child to raise until the end of his days? Whether the two children were from anonymous "johns" or were, in fact, Pat's with one of the working girls, remains an unknown fact to this day.

9

TIPPY THE DOG WOULD LET PEOPLE IN, NOT OUT:
How Our Immigration Policy Should Be

Now, about Tippy the half-Chow dog: he would always let people in our little house in Queens, but he would never let them out. You could come in: he wouldn't bark at all. He smiled, his tongue hung out, but if you tried to leave, he'd attack you. He went crazy! You had to constrain him with an iron chain and then put him in the basement. You'd hear brooms and mops falling down the basement steps. He was like a nutcase dog. So, I had a dog that let people in the house but would never let them out.

I think that that's what we should do with the immigrants in America. "No Middle Eastern immigrants can leave America without a thorough examination by the FBI." You come in, and we don't say a word. You're not getting out though. That's all. You want to leave? Go to the FBI—we'll let you out in a few years, through exam. You can't go out! What are you leaving for all of the sudden? What, the SSI didn't go down. There's religious tolerance here— What are you leaving for, sir? Ah, you're going back to Pakistan to visit your mother? Tell you what: We're going to investigate you until the year 2010. We want to ask you a few questions . . . .

TIPPY DIES AND IS THROWN INTO A GARBAGE TRUCK

The dogs are sleeping. I'm talking with Teddy here: he likes listening to the show and didn't want to go to work today. He wanted to stay here with me, wanted to stay on the couch. He knows tonight I'll cook at home, and he knows when I cook at home he eats like a Roman emperor. Whatever I eat, he gets. If I make a potato, he gets the potato; if I make chicken, he gets the chicken; if I make a bean, he gets the bean. I try to give him more of the beans and vegetables than the flesh along with the "chips" dogs eat today. Had my first childhood dog been fed the high-end dried food of today ("chips") he probably would have lived another 10 years, but they ate garbage in those days. Tippy, they fed him Kennel Ration. I have nothing against the product—I think it was ground up horse hooves or something. We never gave him a grain or a vegetable.

In fact, I once tried to feed that dog a vegetable, and my father yelled at me: "Don't give him a vegetable. They don't eat it!" he said.

"What do you mean, 'They don't eat it'?"

"We're not dogs. They're made for meat, only meat. Don't you dare give him a carrot!"

"Well, he likes it."

"No. Don't give it. You'll poison him. He doesn't have the stomach for it."

The things they didn't know in those days! I tried to slip him a vegetable now and again. I figured he liked it. A horse eats a carrot—why couldn't a dog eat a carrot or a green bean from a plate I didn't want? "No, only the meat, the meat, the meat. He likes the meat. Give him heavy, fatty leftovers, the greasy stuff that even I won't eat. With the bone, give it to him."

Nine years old: dead, a heart attack. Even the dog had a heart attack! Stiff on the rug in Queens: it was a terrible moment. My mother was crying, because a pet is not just an animal after so many years—it's like a retarded child in the house. You come to love him no matter what. Don't think I'm insensitive. It's usually the people who've never lived through it who are the most insensitive. My attackers on the Internet are like a lynching mob—losers in undershirts, bloggers. Lynch mobs, brave with keypads.

So, after nine years, even if he was a little vicious and bit me through to the bone, I came down and I saw the creature stiff on the carpet, unmoving, and my mother's crying:

"What happened? What happened?" I said.

"I don't know, he's dead, he's dead."

"What do you mean he's dead?"

"Look. Look!"

And she touched his legs. He must have been dead for hours because he was already rigid on the rug: "Alright, Ma, get away." I touched him—not directly, because I was afraid he could be in a fit and snap and rip my throat out, because he was a vicious dog. I figured, *Maybe he was knocked out, had an epileptic attack.* So, I didn't touch the whole body right away because it could spring into action and kill me. I touched the foot from a distance so that if he snapped I'd only lose a hand, not my entire arm. I touched the foot and it was rigid. When you touch the pad of the foot of a dead dog, it has the equivalent feeling of a broom, a small broom lying there. So, what am I going to do? I had to call the ultimate authority, but he was still asleep. It was not yet time to go to work. When he woke up, he gave the edict like Caesar: "Alright, it's finished, it's over, boom. Call the garbage men."

"What?" That's what they did! There were no pet cemeteries, with weeping and crying and cremation and jars that people have. I'm soft headed, too. Now, I have a jar with the last dog's ashes, with his picture on the box. The whole world changes: either you go along with it or you wind up crazy. So now, in my living room, I have a box with a dog's ashes in it. I'm sure the ashes in there are not from my dog. I can guarantee they got them from leaves they burned somewhere. Those crooks in those pet crematoriums—like they give you your dog's ashes! "Oh, yeah, here are your dog's ashes." Sure. They probably got it from the park: from a drunk parkee that set the leaves on fire when he fell over in an alcoholic stupor with a cigarette. And they went and told the kid, the half-wit from the neighborhood who worked in the crematorium: "Go get the ashes from the park, from the parkee. Roll him out of the leaves, the bum there, and get the leaves. Bring them in and you're going to set them out in various dishes—the leaves, the burned leaves—and I've got a hundred boxes for you—a hundred!"

"A hundred?"

"Yeah: today, by noon, dummy. Go get the leaves and bring them and stuff them, and then each one, you put a label on: 'Here lies Tippy, the dog that he loved so dear.'"

Inside is a burnt leaf.

But in those days, the garbage men came. In those days ("the sanitation department," as they call it today) the garbage men wore brown suits of a certain hostile fabric. What would you wear if you were in a garbage truck every day? Today garbage men look like Aztecs coming off a truck, with tomahawks. In those days, even the garbage men wore a uniform: it wasn't great—it wasn't designed by Boss. (Boss worked only for Hitler. They made a nice suit for the Nazis. They were Boss designs, if I'm not mistaken—yeah, the one with the big shoulders. They did beautiful uniforms in the '30s: gorgeous.) But today they don't wear uniforms: headbands; bandanas; tomahawks in the back of the garbage trucks; speaking languages with tattoos coming off their tongues. You know, it's a different world, but at least today they don't throw a dog in a garbage truck— that's the thing I'm trying to get at. Who would do that today? Nobody: that would be dog abuse. I watch that show at night, *Animal Police*. They're like saints to me, people in that business. You know, they usually go into poverty neighbor-hoods where they abuse animals, where it's part of the culture. They always say they don't know whose dog it was. "He ran in and I have no idea." The dog was kept with welts and the fur ripped off, barbwire around his neck, and the guy comes and they figure he's coming back from an episode holding up a Seven Eleven. And they say to him, "Hey Jack, is this your dog?"

"No, he just came in here. He jumped the fence."

"What dog? Oh, no, no, never saw him before."

"Look, Jack—"

"No, I don't know whose dog that is—must be my neighbor's dog."

"You getting hostile with me?"

But the guys have a lot of guts in that business with the guns. I really admire them. But, even an animal abuser today wouldn't throw a dog into a garbage truck. What do they do? If one of the dogs finally dies do they use it for Pit Bull practice? Do they bury it?—I don't even know. Do they cook it? What do the poor do with a dead dog? Where do they send it? How do they deal with a dog they snatch from your yard and throw into a Pit Bull ring somewhere? When they're through with it, do they bury it? I really don't know the ins and outs of all this.

SAVAGE'S CHILDHOOD DIET:
Prescription for a Heart Attack

It was 5 o'clock, like clockwork: after a hard day in high school, my mother—God bless her—would put a tray out for me. Oh, was I spoiled. I'm making up for it, though. Now I'm working my butt off. But the tray, the steak, the French Fries—I'm talking French Fries, *steak* French Fries. Here's the diet I had, the healthful diet: breakfast was ham and eggs with a jelly doughnut. Lunch was something light like a meatloaf sandwich with French fries. Dinner was something light, either steak or pot roast with some heavy potato dish, topped off with the health-enhancing cherry-vanilla ice cream and a piece of pie—and maybe a glass of milk to go with it. And this went on for years!

If I were to design an experiment to kill a pig in a laboratory, I'd give him that diet, that cardio-toxic diet, for three months. The pig would roll over and drop dead of an occlusion! I don't know how I'm still kicking! So, diet has something to do with, nothing to do with, or little to do with heart attacks. Now, admittedly, it does because my father, may he rest in peace, died of a heart attack young, and my grandfather did as well. (Well what about great-grandfather back in the Old Country? I was hanging on to the hope that he lived to 103. Oh, I recently learned he, too, died young at 39. Thank you. Three generations dead young. I'm the oldest living Savage in the history of the family! See, every day is like a miracle. And I also know because I spent three decades studying diet and health.)

That's why I went into nutrition; that's why I searched for the secret to longevity for years in the jungles of the South Seas. I'm one of the original ethno-botanists in the field. What I discovered is this: not much is known.

What is known, though, is very important, such as which vitamins you take and in what proportions; which foods you eat and in what proportions; and which herbs to take when. What is known is very interesting and can be lifesaving. I'm a fanatic about mega-nutrition. I'm a fanatic about large doses of vitamins and have been for 30 years. Also, I know to eat onions and garlic and tomatoes and red grapes.

SUNBURN STORY:
Viagra Wasn't Around Then (Thankfully)

When I last got sunburned I felt as though I had lain on the beach at Coney Island. I stay out of the sun because I've had pre-cancerous lesions removed about eight times already in the temple area—from the early years in the sun, when my mother thought getting color was good for me: "Go, go, go. Go in the sun. Get color." I would come back like a lobster: "Good, good. You look good." Women in those days were laying down a cancer in the skin. How did they know? They didn't mean anything by it. They didn't know. They didn't have knowledge of it then.

The same with the food—you know, the heavy food in the morning: eggs and steak for dinner and meatloaf for lunch. Did my mother really know she was killing her son? She wouldn't have done it, I don't think. Do you think the women of her generation were doing it on purpose, to get rid of the males? Sometimes I think that that generation of women was like a female cult: they got married only to have a daughter. The son they could have done without, and the husband. Then Viagra came along. Thank God many of them passed away before that! Could you imagine that? The man loses the ability just at the right point, when the woman doesn't really want him to do that anymore—but now, all of a sudden they have Viagra. A guy could be any age and suddenly he's got a glint in his eye and he's stalking her all over the house—and she doesn't want anything to do with the guy!

It's a curse for many middle-aged women. You know, you think every woman wants to do this? They don't. Most of them leave it behind at a certain point. In the old days, the women gave it up after the second child. They had sex twice: two children and that was it. God didn't want them to enjoy themselves, because they never did enjoy it! Would you have enjoyed it if your husband was a furrier and weighed 350 pounds?

DEAD MAN'S PANTS

Growing up in the Bronx as I did—"the man-child in the Promised Land"—I didn't have many of the luxuries most kids with their hats on backward take for granted today. My father was an immigrant. He worked his fingers to the bone. We simply didn't have the money to afford more than the basics, so, as you might expect, I cherished and took care of the things I had.

As a kid I'd line up my shoes under my bed at night: neat, like in the military. I made sure they were polished, too. I'm sure some shrink today would say I suffered from ADD or other compulsive behavior disorders and should have been put on a regimen of Ritalin.

I wonder what they'd say about the fact that through most of my youth I wore second-hand pants from dead men. Many of the pants I wore as a pre-teen came off of stiffs cut down to fit me.

Don't get me wrong: my father was a good man. He ran a small antique store with mostly 19th century stuff. On the side, at least in the beginning, he sold used goods as well. A man's got to do what a man's got to do to make ends meet, right? Occasionally, he would go to an auction after a man died and buy the entire estate: the clocks, the dishes, the mirrors—whatever the man had—the pants, the shirts, the whole deal. You get the picture.

Back at the store as he sorted the stuff for resale, he'd take a closer look at the suit. Once he got a Hart, Schaffner & Marx suit from a dead man. Now, what's he going to do, toss it in the garbage like they do today? In those days, it wasn't in him to throw out a good worsted fabric. Instead, he brought home the pants to me.

I remember my father called me to the bedroom and showed them to me like the head tailor at Nordstrom's department store. He'd say, "Now, Michael, get a good look at the fabric." I wanted to vomit! I got a migraine because I knew what was coming.

"Take a look at the quality of this fabric—" He's working me like a salesman. He's unrolling the pants on the bed—I can see it to this day! He unrolls it like he's selling me a bolt of hand-woven cloth. He would say, "You can't get fabric like this just anywhere."

I wanted to say, "Of course not, Dad. They only sell stuff like that for men who died."

You know, it was like special clothing for the undertaker.

Even if I had said something, that wouldn't have changed one thing. He'd go downtown and the pants would come back, "fit" for me, you know—shortened, without the legs taken in properly. They ended up baggy, like an Abbott & Costello pair of pants. Even if they had fit me properly, there was something repugnant about the whole idea.

Like I said, I knew how to make do with whatever was at hand. There's an old saying, "The man with no shoes complains until he meets the man with no feet." The fact that I didn't have much more than a place to sleep in my first little apartment after college was OK with me—at least I wasn't wearing dead man's pants.

Little did I know that one day those awful pants would serve as a metaphor for the shift in my political orientation. You might find it interesting that I wasn't always an independent conservative. I was raised in a Democrat, blue-collar home. My dad was a Democrat, my mom was a Democrat—most of my relatives *still* vote Democrat.

To an immigrant family whose parents came of age during the Great Depression, President Franklin Delano Roosevelt was "the Great White Savior." Aside from being the only U.S. President re-elected to office three times, he gained lasting political mileage with the relief that his New Deal offered. As you might expect then, my father used to tell me, "Michael, all I know is, the Democrats are for the little guy and the Republicans are for big business." In a way, his attempt to sell me on the political leanings of the Democratic party was no different than his sales job with the dead man's pants: he was selling me a failed ideology that should have been buried long ago.

So as a young man, not seeing things as clearly as I do now, I voted as my dad did, since I didn't understand politics. As I grew older that view would change completely. The turning point in my thinking can be traced back to my first job out of college as a social worker in the Upper West Side of New York. All of my so-called clients were minorities. Now, I was a good liberal at the time, having had my brain washed at one of the city universities of New York by a whole slew of European immigrants who, instead of kissing the ground when they got here, urinated on the sacred soil and the flag and immediately sought to instill Communist philosophy in the minds of the young.

I didn't know that at the time. I was just a wide-eyed liberal kid with an eye on changing the world. There I was, fresh out of Queens College. Having minored in sociology, I figured I'd take a job as a social worker to save the "oppressed minority." I was always an idealist—I still am, as a matter of fact.

But, the abuses of the welfare system that I saw back then nauseated me and started me on my slow road to recovery. Day after day I found person after person who was working, who had a job, but who claimed they didn't so they could get their government handout. Worse, they knew they were ripping off the welfare system and didn't bat an eye. How can I be so sure these hucksters weren't swindling Uncle Sam? I mean, you could argue that they were *oppressed* and didn't know the rules: not me. At a young age I learned a valuable lesson on how to spot people who smiled to your face while robbing you blind the second your back was turned. The next story about Sam the Butcher is a perfect example.

14

SAM THE BUTCHER

When I was a kid growing up in the Bronx, my Aunt Bea was a lot like my mother in that she practically lived in the kitchen. There was something about that generation of women who took pride in the way they fed their family. Sure, most of the time they served a cardio-toxic diet designed to kill off all of the men before they turned 50, but there was almost always something wonderful in the oven. Day or night, I remember Aunt Bea's home smelled like Thanksgiving morning.

Now in our day, freezer space was limited to ice cubes, so Aunt Bea would buy her meat fresh from Sam the Butcher. This was during a time when the same guy worked the meat counter his whole life. The butcher always knew your name when you came in. He'd order you a special cut of something, maybe a leg of lamb or whatever. Today it's some kid with open sores and a nose ring working the meat counter, and every time you go in it's a different guy. They know you as well as they know where the hamburger they're selling comes from.

I have to say that Sam came from a long line of butchers, probably dating back to the Mongols. He was this stocky Russian—or maybe Ukrainian—man, with oak stumps for arms, a bloodied white apron stretched tight across his belly, and a missing finger. From time-to-time I'd tag along with Aunt Bea for the entertainment value—you know, just to catch a glimpse of Sam wrestling a 300-pound side of beef in the back. We didn't have cable TV in those days. You had to get your entertainment where you could find it.

So, off we went to the market: Aunt Bea would study the fresh cuts of meat behind the refrigerated glass case as if picking out a new diamond ring. Sam would see us through the little window in the swinging door to the meat cutting room. He'd wipe the blood from his beefy hands on his apron as he came out to greet us. He'd mumble something about the fresh this and that, holding up a few meat samples like a Turkish rug salesman offering a closer inspection of the goods. Me? I'm counting the fingers to see if he still had all nine! With a nod, Aunt Bea would point to a roast and ask Sam to cut it into stew-sized pieces. He'd take the meat in the back and return a few minutes later with our selection wrapped in white butcher paper.

We'd get home and she'd toss it in the pot with the spices. I remember one day sitting down to eat and, after one bite, she swore it wasn't the "good stuff" Sam had shown her from the display case. This happened a couple of times, until Aunt Bea got wise to what Sam was doing. It dawned on her that he would sell her on the prime rib up front but when he got to the back, he'd grab something on the order of dog meat. He probably figured she'd never know the difference!

One day I asked, "Aunt Bea, why don't you just follow him into the back to make sure you're not getting gypped?" She did. The next time we went to the market in the heat of a summer day, she put on an extra heavy coat, a scarf, and matching earmuffs, just to stay warm in the back where Sam cut up the beef. When she told Sam that she wanted to follow him into the freezer, he didn't look too pleased. The toothy smile vanished from his face, but what could he do? He shrugged and grunted, "Just don't touch anything."

I had no plans to lose a finger, so I stood there with my arms folded like a mannequin. I'm looking at the meat hooks, the slicers, and the meat cleavers, fascinated by a world I never knew existed. The whole time Aunt Bea studied Sam like a New York City health inspector. This time she made sure we left with the good stuff—and when we got home and she cooked that meat, what a difference!

15

NUTTY FRIEND
HAD CRAZY MOTHER

I had a nutty friend: a real S.O.B., a piece of garbage. He was a miserable rat, even as a kid—a miserable rat because he had a crazy mother who was put on Benzedrine to lose weight. She went to some crazy doctor in Jersey who put her on Speed. She'd come back nuts—I mean crazy! She drove a new pink Cadillac. They had a little more money than everyone else. The father was hardworking. She was a nothing: always on Benzedrine, and a wacko. She was so crazy that one day she took a dog chain and beat herself across the wrists until they were bleeding. When her husband came home at night, after working all day on some delivery route that he owned—he had a franchise, or whatever—she came screaming at him: "Joe, Joe, look what your son did to me! Look what he did to me!" And the father went upstairs and had a fistfight with his son because the crazy mother said that the son did this to her wrists, when she did it herself!

Can you believe this kind of situation? But this old boyhood friend was a rat before that, and he's still a rat. But, he was a good friend of mine when I was in the fifth grade. Since I was sort of a mischievous child, naturally I sought out the more mischievous of the students: those who fidgeted the most; those who had the brightest eyes and never listened to the teacher—they were my kind of people. Today they would put us into Ritalin therapy and turn us into robots. I wouldn't be on the radio today; I'd be an accountant somewhere in a prison. I'd be counting underwear for a prison to make sure that the underwear didn't get stolen!

But, the long and short of it is the crazy mother—but her madness didn't excuse him for being nuts. As years went on, two of the boys in the neighborhood became famous rock 'n roll singers—two from Queens; I won't mention their names. One had a big hit at 13 years old. He was always more mature than us. He had a 19-year-old girlfriend—I never understood why. Maybe it was his pompadour. The rest of us were still dreaming. Eventually he went and did a tour, this musician, in Japan, at age 14. Dropped out of high school on this one song that was a huge hit, so he goes to Japan on a big tour. The Japanese always liked American rock 'n roll-ers.

Years later he's on his behind, and he's got nothing. So, he becomes a U.S. postman. The same rock 'n roll-er—who had a Jaguar XK140 before anyone could even drive such a machine; cuffs that stood out of his jacket; the pompadour —became a postman. There's nothing wrong with being a postman, but, you know, you start out as a rock 'n roll-er and you end up as a postman: that's a pretty hard road, you know what I'm saying? It's better to start out as a postman and end up a rock 'n roll star.

16

CONEY ISLAND WAX FIGURES

Going back now to the bad kid whose mother beat herself on the arm: we liked to go all over New York by subway. When we were 12 or 13 we went everywhere in Manhattan. We would cruise down in the bowels of the basement of the subways on 42nd Street, where sleazy merchants were selling soft-core porno magazines. You'd see the old geezers there lining up, looking at the magazines. We'd try to look and —"Kid, get out of here, get out of here"— that kind of thing.

We also used to like to go to Coney Island. They had weird exhibits, mannequins of wax figures. Some of them were frightening. One was of George Metesky, the "mad bomber" of the subway. They were so life-like that, if you were 12 and you had just been on a New York subway car for an hour and stared at one of those exhibits, the guy looked like he was going to come out of the cell and strangle you.

Well, adjacent to that mad bomber display there was another guy: this scared me. To this day I have nightmares about him. It showed a guy who kidnapped and dismembered girls and women. He was really bad, this one. He looked like an ordinary Joe: white guy, ordinary guy. It was a mad time in New York City. Girls were being found dismembered. Finally, they tracked this nut down to a chicken farm in New Jersey. They found a corpse in a trunk under the bed.

This exhibit in Coney Island shows this guy reconstructed in wax in a little room in the back of a chicken farm with a dismembered girl's body in a trunk, and he's got blood on his feet, with a blank stare at you—and they show you the feet and the hands and blood. Today they could never ever display this, but life then was richer as a result. They had freak shows in those days. A genuine freak show is not so bad: the freak had a job. If I went to Ringling Brothers and Barnum & Bailey, I didn't go for the horse or the elephant—I went for the freak show in the back: the one-breasted man; the half-bearded woman (in other words, the people who today have become politicians). In my day they were in the back room of Ringling Brothers and Barnum & Bailey.

Freak shows: half-man, half-woman; half human; half amoeba. It was wonderful. I liked the whole thing: you eat the popcorn, you walk around, you gape at the freak, you thank God that you're not like them. But, the truth of the matter is, you think, *Well, they're exploiting the freak.* But those who worked in those shows did not feel "exploited." They made a good living; they were around other abnormal people; they had a little world, a social world; they had sex, some of them, with each other. Today, what? They sit at home watching television on welfare? You think that's better for a freak?

So, there's something to be said for going back to the America of the 1950s. Please do me a favor. Don't bring up the Civil Rights Act. America of the 1950s with a Civil Rights Act—can we move on now? It was a better country. OK, everyone's equal, but give me back the freak show and give me back the exhibit of the guy that a kid could see was totally crazy. Why should a kid see that? A kid should see that in order to understand there are dangers in the world. Certain people are really crazy and bad.

17

HALF-MAN, HALF-WOMAN
IN LONG BEACH

I've got to tell you about the half-man, half-woman from Long Beach. As I've said, my dad had a small antique store. He sold clocks and figures and statutes, mainly 19th century French collectibles. Some of it was very good. Among his many customers was a circus performer in the freak show of Ringling Brothers. He had a breast on one side and on the other side he didn't; half a beard (which he probably shaved to create). After work, he was just a regular person who lived in a house in Long Beach, Long Island.

After work Dad delivered his own sales—he didn't have a delivery boy. I was a kid, and I'd go along on the ride, whether it'd be in the DeSoto or the model '62 Cadillac, with the statues in the back. We'd pull up late at night because this guy didn't like to come out during the day. I'll never forget this as long as I live: the circus guy, the half-man, half-woman.

Ring ring, "Who's there?" blah, blah, blah . . . .

So the guy opens the door, but he can't open the door all the way; he can only open it a crack. Why? He has to pull the door and push stuff: the house is now littered with art objects, in no particular order—hundreds of statues and paintings on the floor; nothing hung right. He would buy one beautiful thing after another and just randomly put it on the floor, like in a warehouse.

Why was that? Nobody knew, but I figured it out. I was a kid who thought about these things on those long rides out to Long Island and the long rides back—those long winter nights over the Williamsburg Bridge in the car with the sound of grated metal underneath the tires as your car went over it, looking down at the ships that came back from the Korean War, the LSTs in the Brooklyn Navy

Yard. I figured out what it was: this guy was a freak and ugly in his own mind, so he compensated for his ugliness by buying beautiful objects. He needed to surround himself with beautiful things as much as possible, in a compulsive way. I did not go into psychiatry because I didn't want to subject myself to people's problems, but I know what people are all about—including the half-man, half-woman in Long Beach.

18

THE CHESTNUT MAN

There were a lot of crazy people in those days on the streets. Today there are, too, but they're holding microphones and they're working for the media. Here was one of our subway rides: cold, nasty, miserable, snowy winter day; slush, 11 years old, dressed up like a snowman—one of those days where mist is coming out of your mouth it is so cold; your face is red, your hands could freeze if you take a glove off. I loved that weather. There was a bimmie who sold chestnuts outside the Museum of Natural History. I loved going to see the mastodon; I liked the gem collection.

I didn't know it in those days, but those trips shaped a lot of my future, by showing me the greatness of our culture. When I'd go to the Museum of Natural History as a kid and see exhibits of a natural scene from the Fiji Islands, with birds, little did I know that years later I would actually seek out that kind of thing in my life professionally. Shaped in part by the great cultural institution of the Museum of Natural History—no doubt about it.

Of course, this is all lost today on the Islamo-fascists whose ancestors burnt down the library at Alexandria. Lost, too, on the TV generation, and by the Internet and the iPod. I don't know what these children are going to become. What is their dream? What kind of dreams do children have?—I haven't any idea! It's very sad that children have so few dreams. I will come back to the Chestnut Man, but I have to tell you of another related event.

After work I went on one of my one-hour walks around downtown San Francisco. I needed to burn off energy. Hat tilted low, collar up, anonymous; no one knows me, till I open my mouth. Then heads turn, so I don't say anything. I like to go and look into restaurants and bars: I like seeing people going home, and the hustle and bustle. A good conclusion of the day for me is to see the humanity in this beautiful city of San Francisco. So, at one of the places I stop, a boutique hotel, there's a bar scene. I like to see the hubbub. I never liked the bar scene when I was young and I'm not in the bar scene, but I like to watch it, sitting in a lobby. So, I'm sitting in the lobby on a chair, and in the bar there are hundreds of people: kids in their 30s. Everyone's a "7" in there, which is actually why it's more fun. They probably go home with each other—the 7s. The 9s and 10s go home to psychopathic behavior. The 7s at least go home with each other because they don't think they're God.

So, the place is packed with 7s, and I'm sitting in a chair in the lobby and watching the comings and goings. Every girl that comes through the lobby pulls out a cell phone, and even though they're alone, the girls are looking at their cell phones—talking, making believe that they have somebody they're waiting for. That's the latest gimmick. They think somebody's buying into it, that if you pull out a cell phone it means your date's late and you're there and you're busy and you're popular. And they're all staring at a non-existent text message—they're staring as if inside a fortune teller's crystal, to see if they can find a visage of the truth inside their little instrument. If I were from another planet looking in I'd say, "What kind of madness is this? What kind of species is this in which young females who are searching for husbands to settle down and have children with are walking around with a device in their hands? Instead of talking to a man, they're talking to this device in their hands and staring at it as if it's the Holy Grail itself!"

Now, to go back to the chestnuts in the open fire: We're outside the museum, freezing slushy cold, and one of these bimmies is selling chestnuts. They're delicious—man, they roast them out there! Do they still do that? I don't even know if they allow them anymore. I'm with my friend: we're 11, and the bum says to us, "Hey, you guys—." He talked in a weird voice; he was a big guy. He looked like a roughneck but a little lower class than that even—a little nuttier. He says, "Hey, you kids want to see pictures of girls?" So, right away, I knew he was a dangerous guy. So, we play him along.

"Yeah, yeah, yeah. Where do you have those pictures?"

"You kids come with me, come with me. It's only a subway ride. I'll show you those pictures." We didn't go with him because we knew he was a pervert. How did we know? Because we were allowed to ride the subway at 11 p.m. instead of being locked up behind a Web page.

19

ONE-ARMED FRANK

D id I ever tell you about One-armed Frank? My father knew a guy with one arm. I don't know how the guy became one-armed but, you know— you didn't know a lot of people with one arm in those days. Even today: I guess you don't know one-armed people because they have fake arms. He had the arm sewn up in a suit. Nobody hid reality in those days. Today it's like, "Oh, yeah, he's normal. He's just like us." In those days, it was "One-armed Frank." Today, it's like, "Oh, he's better than normal. Man, he's special"—like if you have one arm, you're better than a guy with two arms today. You know what I mean? If you have no arms and no legs, you're superman in the politically correct world!

But in those days, if you were missing an arm, that's what you were named. Whatever your anomaly was, that was your name. It made it easier for the average person to remember everybody. So, One-armed Frank was a very sweet guy, but he had sick breath. Now I want to tell you, there are bad breaths and then there are very bad breaths—then there are medicinal problems. This one had to be solved with a medicine that hasn't been invented yet! I remember one winter my old man was dropping Frank off at his home. Frank was in the passenger seat and I sat in the back. It was minus four degrees out, but we had to ride with all the windows open. Did you ever meet a person like this? Whenever he spoke the car filled with a nauseous fume.

"Are we going past the Trunz meat factory?"

"No. We're not in Williamsburg."

"Did we run over a small furry creature that got caught in the muffler and the smell shot up through the floorboard. Did I step on something?"

"No, it's Frank talking."

20

LOUIE AND HIS CRAZED MONKEY

I once read a story about monkeys invading the capital of India. Just weeks before, the deputy major died after falling off a balcony while fighting off a pack of monkeys. The story I read said that the animals were attacking again, with one woman seriously hurt and two dozen other people given first-aid in the East Delhi neighborhood.

So the monkeys are out of control—rogue monkeys running into residences. I guess if I go on with the story I'll be accused of simeophobia—and I'd be liable to face a boycott from some monkeys around the globe, and I can't afford that because if the monkeys were to boycott my products there'd be no conservatives left to buy them, I suppose.

Liberalism turns all animals "cute": a bear is "cute", a monkey is "cute." Monkeys are dangerous, with big teeth! This reminds me of the story of "Louie and His Monkey." We go back now: ladies and gentlemen, put on your resting caps. We're going back in time. We're going back to the Lower East Side of New York.

Dad owns a small antiques mart. Little ol' Michael is cleaning bronzes in the back and there's Louie the Drunk from the bowery. He wasn't a bum—he worked, but he was an alcoholic. Dad would have him in on the weekends and he'd clean the bronzes—and whatever else he did down there. I loved Louie. Louie was a great guy.

You've got to understand, this guy was an alcoholic of the old school: skinny like a rail; white guy; smoked unfiltered cigarettes—but one of the nicest guys on earth. He wore the rubber apron. He cleaned bronze statues with cyanide! Then, of course, I took over because Dad wanted cheap child labor, and where else was he going to get it? As a result, I got to know Louie over the years. He taught me various things. Once we had Louie over to the house—I'll never forget it—I was so proud that my father took this guy, who I liked, all the way out to Queens and invited him to dinner. I don't know what came over him. Maybe it was Thanksgiving. Louie had dinner with us at the table, and the guy was surprisingly erudite. He knew things.

After dinner we did games, and Louie the Drunk showed me how to bend nails. He showed me mind over matter by taking a nail and showing me that if you put your thumbs on the center and pull back with your other fingers and focus your mind on it and keep up the pressure, the nail will bend! I was shocked because I was a skinny kid with little hands—and I bent the nail! He taught me mind over matter—but it is all molecular, as a result of constant pressure producing heat, which permits you to bend the nail.

I learned that in life it's the same thing: it's all willpower. Now there's another element to the story. So, Louie is this king of a guy, interesting but an alcoholic. Years go by. He lives alone in Williamsburg. In those days Williamsburg was a slum, zero—you know, oil-cloth city; leftover apartments from the last century. No one wanted to be there but the poor. So he lives there alone. He's very lonely. He gets a monkey—he wants a monkey! Now, nobody in those days had a monkey. Dogs, yes. Cats, yes. Who had a monkey in those days? Louie gets a monkey. Louie didn't just get a spider monkey, one of the skinny little monkeys. Louie got a wooly monkey. Now, wooly monkeys are really strong: they've got a chest on them and strong hands. Louie is in love with this monkey. For a couple of months they're inseparable. Wherever he goes, there's the monkey: the monkey's on his shoulder, while he's cleaning, and he's happy.

Now Louie was the kind of guy that if he went to a bar on the Lower East Side he'd throw money in the jukebox, and he would whistle and sing and buy everyone drinks until he was broke. I remember the name of that bar to this day: Hammel and Korn. Whatever money he made from my father, he'd take it and two minutes later he'd be in the bar. Later, he'd stumble out into the street. If a car brushed him, he'd sleep on the bowery and didn't care. He lived for the booze— that was it—but he had a heart of gold.

So, Louie gets the wooly monkey. Finally he has someone to fill his empty nights. As I said, they were inseparable. Well, as time went on, we got a call: Louie's in the hospital. He's in critical condition. "What?" The monkey went crazy in his apartment, attacked him, almost ripped him to pieces. He suffered for six months in the hospital. I don't know which hospital, probably Bellevue because that's where they all wound up. The monkey went at him—you don't know what a monkey's like when it goes crazy. You try to stop an enraged monkey without a weapon! He ripped his neck; he ripped his face; he ripped his arms; he ripped his legs; he ripped his crotch; he ripped his behind.

Louie was ripped up pretty badly, but we learned that during the fight he grabbed his pet and threw it out the window. It just shows you that if he hadn't done it he'd be dead today. A liberal probably would have tried to talk to the monkey, but Louie knew that the instincts had to kick in: it was him or the monkey. He decided that it was better him than the monkey. He didn't consult the liberal playbook on how to deal with a crazed monkey—he just fought with it and killed it. I think that's what the bottom line is here, but the point is, even a lonely drunk needs companionship at night. In his case, he found the monkey. It was probably the right thing for him to do.

But it goes back to the story I opened with, which is that the monkeys are rampaging in India. Rogue monkeys are breaking into houses, even into the house of the daughter of the ruling Congress party. They broke into the Indian parliament. Trouble boiled over in late October when the city's deputy mayor fell to his death, while driving away monkeys from his home. He waves a stick to scare them away, tumbles over the edge, and boom! He drops dead—falls off the balcony and dies.

So, right now you can see that Louie was a pioneer, in a way, in the sense that he understood that monkeys were dangerous long before they did in India, when they turned it into a sacred animal. That's the "Louie and His Monkey" story on "The Savage Nation." The bottom line is, don't get a monkey as a pet: they're wild animals.

LIKED WALTER CRONKITE *and* PURGATORY OF MANHOOD BY CYANIDE

Who did I actually like in mainstream news? Let me just run on this for a minute. I did like Walter Cronkite because he had a deep voice and a mustache. He reminded me of an Italian dentist that I knew in the Bronx. You always had to behave yourself when you were around guys with mustaches like that because they could do weird things to you if you didn't. Cronkite was a very authoritative man, and how he presented the world is how I thought the world was.

I might be eating steak and French Fries and cherry-vanilla ice cream on a TV tray, building up my negative cardiac profile, while Dad was working. I'd be watching Walter Cronkite. I had no idea what he was talking about. See, kids don't really know what the news is—nor does the average adult really pay that much attention. I think we give media people too much power by thinking people really listen to their every word. Every time they put out another fib I become incensed: "Oh, look what they said; look at the phony poll about Obama!" But the fact is that they don't have that much direct influence on the average person. I get excited because I can see what they're doing, but do you?

Dad would walk in at 6:30, white from a day in the store. He might just have fought his way home through a snowstorm in his big, green DeSoto, and here is his No. 1 son getting fat, watching television, eating steak and cherry-vanilla ice cream. He's starving and there's no food for him. I don't have to tell you what flashed through his eyes, my eyes, my mother's eyes—even the dog's eyes! He never thought I'd amount to anything. The arguments we would have!

"You're ruining the kid. Look what you're doing. You're making him soft. You got to make a kid hard," he used to yell. "Look what you're doing to the kid: you're making him a weakling. He'll never amount to anything. He's soft. Look at him over there eating that steak and ice cream." He was probably starving at that point. He got home with the slush and galoshes, snow over the top, and his worst nightmare came true: his wife was catering to his son.

The guy comes back from the hunt, and what's going on in the cave? The woman he is married to is cooking for the child, who has done nothing that day but go to school. And look at girls! So, it was soon thereafter that the whole "soft life" came to an end: no more ice cream. No steak. No TV trays. I was forced to go into his store's basement on Ludlow Street to clean bronzes. That's the beginning of my purgatory and my manhood.

I was cast down into the cellar where I used cyanide solution to clean bronze statues of their gorgeous patina. The statues were gorgeous. I learned a lot about art because I stared at them all day long. Now, you may say, "What do you know about art?" I know quality from junk, artistry from fakery: the rest is a matter of taste. So these figures would come in with a brown or black patina, which is the result of oxidation over time. The patina was sublime, but the nouveau who were buying the figures to turn them into lamps wanted them to glitter like gold. Underneath the patina was the original bronze metal.

"I'll take that, I'll turn it into a lamp, mount the thing," blah, blah, blah . . . . They'd buy it and a certain number would be left for the weekend that I'd have to clean down in the basement. Down into the dirty, horrible, dank dungeon, filled with huge old wine barrels; a toilet from hell; no mirror on the wall, except a shattered shard speckled from the acid that hit it. I'm down there from a young age with a toothbrush, scrubbing away at the patina.

I don't really know if the cyanide was that bad. If it was, I'd be dead by now, I think. Perhaps it protected me from something: "Dad, explain to me how I can use cyanide, since I understand from basic chemistry that they use cyanide balls at San Quentin? They put a guy in the chair and strap his head over the bucket and the pellets drop in. Then the gas comes up, and he's dead in a few seconds. Why would you put me in a basement with cyanide pellets to clean bronzes?"

Here's the answer now—this is right out of the Bible. I couldn't believe it took me 30 years to figure this out! This was a repetition of Abraham and Isaac. See, Abraham picked up the knife and God said, "Slay your son."

He didn't even ask, "My son? You sure you mean my son?"

"Your son. I want him slain."

"Alright, I'm a good guy. I'll kill my son for you."

He grabs the kid, grabs him by the neck—like an Islamo-fascist—and is about to cut his throat when God says, "I was just kidding. I was only testing you."

Now, no one ever talked about what that did to Isaac. The father he trusted suddenly grabs him by the neck and wants to cut his throat. You know, all you hear about is "Abraham was so loyal and he listened to God." But what did it do to Isaac? It drove him crazy! He never trusted anyone after that. His own father wanted to cut his throat because he was listening to someone in the sky!

So now I'm in the basement and he says to me, "You're going to clean bronzes because you're going to be a man; I'm going to make you tough; you gotta do something; blah, blah, blah. And you're going to use these pellets. Here's a big barrel of them. I get them from a chemical supply store. You drop them in water, and then you dip in your brush and wash the bronze and the black comes off and it looks shiny again." The customer wants the shiny statue for a lamp.

So, I say to him, "How do you know it's not going to kill me?"

Here's what Abraham says to me, I mean in the modern day story: "Because there's a potassium salt of the cyanide and a sodium salt of the cyanide." But he doesn't tell me which one kills and which one dissolves patina—which is exactly why I went into science and medicine and chemistry, to find out whether he was trying to knock me off or not.

Nobody else would do this except Louie from the bowery, the one with the monkey. We'd get rubber gloves on up to our elbows and drop these white pellets into water to turn it into a cyanide solution. Then we'd take the brush and rub the figure until the patina came off the bronze. I'm rubbing: it would take you an hour or two to do each statue. Rub, rub—I'm a kid. I'm rubbing, and what I'm thinking about is where I'm going that night: I'm going out on a date or to hang out with my friends, or I'm going to the movies.

Meanwhile, my face would be blotched, and I'm rubbing and cleaning in what's like a Dickens' basement. So, I got into high school chemistry and I told my teacher what I was doing: I was using cyanide balls. My father had a huge chemical supply—it was not used for anything but this. I said to the teacher that I used these cyanide balls for a cleaning solution.

He said, "What? It's poisonous! But don't get worried. There's a sodium cyanide and there's a potassium cyanide salt." Now, to this day, I don't know which one kills you.

If you're a doctor reading this, or a trained scientist, I want you to think about what I'm going to say. Is it possible that inhaling the fumes that didn't kill me outright in some way mitigated against the oxidation of fatty foods powering through my arteries? I have a pet theory that in some way, although it blotched my face, it built up my immunity to something—I know it did.

22

END OF DAY GLASS

I remember learning this when I was a kid in my father's antique store: let me tell you what end of day glass is. Don't you sometimes enjoy a multitude of stories without the distraction of a logical connection? End of day glass is similar to stream-of-consciousness storytelling. Some of the most colorful glass is variegated glass. You know, all sorts of colors were in those vases made with variegated glass.

"Dad, what's that?"

"Well, Michael, that's end of day glass."

"What is that, Dad?"

"Well, at the end of the day in the glass shop, they have different colors that were left over from the various things they were making, and they melted it and then put it all together and it became this beautiful, multicolored glass. All the different colors were melted down and made into a thing called 'end of day glass.'"

My dad knew so much—never went to college, but he was worldly-wise and knew reality. I was blessed. Not saying that if you go to college you don't know reality; I'm not an elitist nor am I anti-elitist. I'm highly educated. Not everybody who has a higher education is an idiot: let's not get carried away with these categories. But, my dad was a smart guy who happened to not go to college. He could always surprise me with his knowledge. I was very lucky in that way.

23

THE NYMPHO
IN ALLEY POND PARK

I was about 16 years old, Queens, New York. One of the girls in the crowd, she was that way: a nymphomaniac. It was a cold winter's evening and a group of five or six guys took her in a car to Alley Pond Park and had their way with her. I was one of the guys in the car, and I did not want my way with her. In fact, I felt bad for her. I didn't know what to do. I was the idiot, sensitive kid in the back who was laughed at.

"Hey, it's your turn."

I said, "No, I just don't want to do this—there's something wrong here."

So after these guys—these pigs, these animals, most of whom wound up working in the garment center selling clothing; some I think went into the television business; one went into the record business—got through with her, the car took her back to her house. Here's the whole crux of the story: it's not like I'm laughing about "the nymphomaniac in the car." Car pulls up in front of her house. She lived in a nice house, and her father was waiting for her on the lawn of the house with an overcoat in his arms. The guys basically threw her, disheveled and half naked, out of the car. Laughing, they sped away. I turned around and saw the father walking up to her to cloak her and cover her nakedness with the overcoat.

Now, there's so much in this story that needs to be discussed: what a father! What a great father he was. Now, you'd think a father would scream, "You filthy slut, you! How dare you!" Or, he'd come at the car and hit the guys. He didn't do either, did he? He lived with what was. He knew who his daughter was and what her proclivities were.

I don't know how she wound up—maybe she turned out OK. A lot of people go through these phases, and they—on the woman's side—can straighten out. I don't know what they become: maybe yoga instructors later on in life; or, if they're males and suffer from satyriasis, they become president—like Bill Clinton. If they suffer the equivalent of nymphomania in a male, it's called satyriasis, and that can make you into a wonderful ACLU lawyer in some cases. In either case, that's the story of the nymphomaniac in Alley Pond Park.

24

LOVE BY THE SEWER PLANT

S hall I tell you the story of "Love by the Sewer Plant"? Remember the song "I Only Have Eyes For You" sung by The Flamingos? We're talking Route 42. We're talking '56, '57. We're talking a sewer plant. We're talking about love by the sewer plant: first love by the sewer plant.

Now, this girl was so beautiful that people stopped as she went by, to marvel at her. We were at a small hotel owned by a former boxer—a pugilist, a real tough guy. If he got into an argument with anyone who worked for him and they got smart, he beat them up and threw them off the property: that type. Everyone was terrified of him, an old school, New York Jewish kind of street-fighter type.

So, he ruled his little hotel with an iron fist. Because he was tough, things ran right. Nothing ever went wrong: no one robbed cutlery, no one talked back. So, any-way, I'm a kid, 15 years old, and boom: it's "love by the sewer plant." We crossed the road to walk down to the Neversink River, to make out. The water was so cold that when you waded across your feet turned blue.

My uncle had a new Plymouth Fury, so I remember the time. This girl was so stunningly gorgeous, just really beautiful, and the theatre companies would come through—they had entertainment in these hotels, in small theatres that they called "casinos,"—for a night of entertainment. Sometimes they'd have a come-dian who was terrible, a juggler, or a balloon man doing cheap acts—in other words, schlocky entertainment.

Nevertheless, they thought they were artists; you've got to understand that. Even though they were schlocky entertainers—let's say they could paint velvet paintings—they were still painters. In their minds, they were Van Goghs. They were theatrical and everyone else was boring. In other words, they were the artists—they understood beauty. So one day a group of these entertainers came around and just stared at this girl. They came running up to her as if I wasn't there. I was holding her hand and walking with her. We were just kids. One of them said, "Man, I wanted you to see this girl! This is the girl I was telling you about." They looked at her like she was a specimen of biblical beauty.

Where are you going to go when you're a kid and you've got nowhere to go? So, we took a walk down the hill. It was a long slope down to the river where there was a sewer treatment plant, which occasionally, as you well know, doesn't smell that good. Kids don't care, though. They can over-ride anything, particularly when the lust hits them. So, we two kids walk down the hill, cross the river, roll up the dungarees, take off our shoes—our legs were blue—and we have a little moment of passion together. It was my first moment of passion and not exactly on the level of a complete moment of passion—but, for me, it was the first of that type. So now I'm star-struck. Coming back to my little cottage, the knees of my pants were soaking wet. The pants were soiled elsewhere so I let my shirt tails out, calling, "Hi Mom, what's to eat?" as I hurried my clothing into the wash basket.

There were not enough stars in the sky that night, in the black sky, the billions of stars, to equal the passion that I had for the world. I thought I could literally reach out and grab a star and fly away—that's how phenomenal I felt that evening!

But then of course, as you well know, nothing like that lasts. So, what I'm getting at with the story, is that it was by a sewer plant, and there's nothing more to it. Now imagine some John Coltrane, because there's no more to the story that I care to tell. If I tell anymore it will become a pantomime, and I don't want to embarrass myself with a pantomime of something that was quite beautiful. This story ends abruptly. Good jazz ends abruptly.

25

FAT AL'S TUNA

I was 17 and working as a bus boy at Schenk's Paramount Hotel up in the Catskill Mountains of New York. I'd work there every summer to pay for college—the hours were gruesome. We'd work from five in the morning until midnight. You had to get up at five to prep the breakfast, then you worked the early bird, then you worked the breakfast. You weren't out of the dining room until 10; you were sweaty and dirty. Then you had to be back at 11:30 for the crowd to pour in for lunch—and you had to smile at them! They'd usually rip a bill in half and say to you, "Hey kid, my name is George Shapiro. Let me tell ya something. See this $20 bill? Me and my family are gonna be here for two weeks. Take this half of the bill. . . . "—I promise this really happened!—He'd say, "Give us good service, I'll give you the other half."

Anyway, then you'd work the lunch rush. You'd clean up only to get ready to serve dinner. You wouldn't get out of there until nine and be back at midnight for the "snack". That's the way it worked. It was something out of Dickens.

You know, kitchens and how they worked fascinated me: how they could serve so many different meals so quickly. I loved to see the guys carrying the trays and the guys screaming at them from the back, "Watch out, moron!" It was awesome—the running, the hustling, the bustling, and all the yelling.

I remember in the kitchen there was a guy we called Fat Al. He was the breakfast and lunch cook, a fat Italian guy, maybe 400 pounds of blubber. Underneath the blubber was solid iron. He had a neck on him like a tree stump! He'd wear a bandana around his neck and on top of his head, and he'd sit with a cigarette hanging out the side of his mouth as he cooked. I don't know how old he was—could have been 38. To me, he looked 90.

One day, old Fat Al called me over. He said, "Hey kid, come here. I'll show you how to make the tuna." As I watched, his cigarette dangled from his mouth over the bowl. I'll never forget how Fat Al didn't use a Cuisinart to mix things—you know, with the stainless steel blades that all the fancy chefs use today. No, Fat Al mixed stuff with his big mitt. He'd be up to his armpit in the tureen, mixing the tuna and seasonings, his arm going around and around in the bowl.

At one point he said, "All right, kid, throw in the Mayo." So I'm throwing in the jars of Mayo. He keeps mixing it with his hairy arm in the bowl. I'm saying to myself, "Some of the hair's gotta be in the tuna!" Of course, his cigarette ashes were falling from his mouth, too, so that's when I decided to take my chances and say something:

I said, "Excuse me, Al. What about the ashes getting in there?"

He said, "Never mind. It gives it flavor."

With that exchange in the back of my mind, I figured that if I had said anything to my supervisor—like why in the world is the government handing out checks to people who refuse to work faster than Santa on Christmas Eve—she'd probably say, "Don't worry, Michael: this is their entitlement." By the time my supervisor was done rattling off a list of "entitlements," the total "owed" to the welfare-cheats for furniture was something like what I would have earned in a year. I was supposed to authorize a check to Mr. and Mrs. Whomever to furnish their welfare apartment so they could lead a standardized life. Me? I went home to a mattress on the floor and two orange crates—and I was the professional with a college degree!

That's when I knew the system was broken. That's when I knew the system was sick.

26

SAVAGE'S MOTHER CALLS
WHILE SHOW IS ON

Now, why is someone calling me in the middle of a show? Don't they know I'm on the air? They don't know I'm on the radio? After all these years people bother me during show time, 7:10 in the evening on the East Coast! What are they, crazy? Now, let me answer the phone right here on the air.

"Joe's Pizza. Who is this? Who is it?" Yep, would you believe it? It was my mother. I had to hang up on her. This is a stunner for me. I'll have to call her during the break. She was shocked when I said "Joe's Pizza."

That was an absolutely real call, I swear to you. The day is crazy, the weather is nutty. Things are blowing around. Went from summer to winter here in the Bay area.

27

REMEMBERING CHILDHOOD DOOR AND LOCKS:
Mothballs and Mother Savage

I was lying in bed last night, about three in the morning, when I started to laugh out loud. I rarely laugh out loud in bed because the dog will think I'm crazy. I started to laugh because the thought occurred to me that, when I was a youth and still living with my parents—maybe I was 16 or 17—I remember coming home after a night of carousing with my friends to that little attached brick house with the rock solid front door and turning that lock. There's something about that door—I've never been able to duplicate the doors they had on houses in those days, or the locks. When you turned the tumbler on those locks, you heard the tumbler turn. You felt like Willie Sutton breaking into a bank, it was such a wonderful sound. And the minute the door opened, mothballs and heat assailed all of your senses.

My mother kept the heat up at around 90 degrees in the winter. She put mothballs in every article of clothing in every closet and then scattered more balls on the floor of the closet. You've got to picture this house: an attached house, so to speak—a row house, in other words. Think of a British movie from the '50s; remember those movies and the attached brick houses? Now think Queens, '50s, post-war attached houses—small, maybe 20 feet wide. The lot was 100 feet long. The house was maybe 20 feet by 60 feet. It was very narrow, but to me it was like a palace after where we had come from.

So, mothballs were in every clothing bag, every closet. In the hallway when you went in, you had to walk sideways into the vestibule. I didn't care that it was a small hallway—at least I had a hallway! To the immediate right of the hallway was a closet door. She had mothballs in there, in every piece of clothing, and a vacuum cleaner was jammed in there too! Everything was neat, don't get me wrong—nothing was jumbled—but in every coat, a mothball. God bless her, the woman had a phobia about bugs. I don't know what the mothballs were for: to keep the fur? I don't know.

But, I used to say, "Ma, it's so hot in here. My eyes are smarting from the mothballs."

"Never mind, I like the heat," she'd say, and that was the end of the discussion. There was no discussing at that point. She would have been great at talk radio, my mother. She closed the argument down just by answering what you started to say. There was no discussion—"Never mind, I like the heat." That was it. There was no arguing, no reasoning. Perfect caller—actually, perfect host.

But, what was the thing with the mothballs? I don't understand. I'm starting to think there may be a health benefit to mothballs that we don't yet understand. That's when I broke into laughter in bed, and Teddy, my poodle, rolled over and looked at me like I was crazy.

Indianapolis, Scott: You're on "The Savage Nation." Go ahead, please.

SCOTT: Hi, Michael. Your mama Savage was on to something with the mothballs. She probably never saw a mouse or anything in her house as long as she kept those mothballs going.

SAVAGE: She hated mice. She was terrified of them—but she was trying to kill the moths. How did she kill the mice?

SCOTT: My mother and grandmother did the same thing, and they never had mice in their houses. According to a home remedies book that my mother had, one of the chemicals in the mothballs is a deterrent to mice.

SAVAGE: You're kidding! She was terrified of mice. She was a strong woman and not very frightful, but terrified of mice. I remember once we were in a rented cottage in the mountains, and a mouse got in the cottage. There were no mothballs there because it was a summer place. She didn't have any up in the mountains. Man, she jumped up on a chair with a broom, screaming at the mouse!

Why are women afraid of mice? I don't want to go into the Freudian right now—I'm sorry. Thanks for the call.

28

MY SILENT BROTHER

I remember the day they gave Jerome away. My uncle Murray was crying like a baby in front of the South Bronx tenement we lived in. All the neighbors were out watching; think Calcutta, a Satyajit Ray film. The little blond boy with blue eyes was only five. I was seven; my sister was nine. He was packed off like an animal to live and suffer and die in silence, alone in one New York snake pit after another. The "doctor" told my parents he would only live to age seven—he lied. The great man also told my parents, "It would be better for the other children," to give him away. This created a lifetime of shame and guilt for me. I became emotionally responsible for discarding this helpless little boy, who I loved more than anyone else in my entire life!

How I loved my little defenseless brother, born blind and deaf and unable to hold himself up! All those times I would secretly sneak into the kitchen where he sat propped up in his high chair:

"Don't go in there. Don't bother him. He can't see you or hear you anyway." But I would go and whistle to him, and his eyes would light up! I would see a sparkle where the "doctor" said there was only darkness. So I knew he could hear me whistling to him and see my shadow or smell me. He was alive, and they were told to exile him, for my sake!

After he was gone, the little apartment became more silent than when the silent boy was there. For years afterward I would sneak into the dresser drawer where my mother preserved his little clothing and eyeglasses (they tried to see if they would work.) I would hold one of his laundered shirts to my nose, pressing the fabric right into my nostrils to glean a few molecules of his scent. I even wore his eyeglasses, making the room all blurry. My brother! They took him away.

For decades (not just the two years she was told he would live) my poor mother took buses and subways all the way out to Staten Island or up to Poughkeepsie to visit him. Sometimes my sister went with her, but mostly she went alone. The new clothing she brought for him, on each and every visit, was never seen on him. They wheeled him out in the same institutional sackcloth. She would come home wrecked and hopeless for days afterward. The arguments between my parents started to get very bad after this, with both blaming each other, when it was really the doctor's fault. There was some kind of medication given during pregnancy that damaged my brother's central nervous system during development.

Finally, after about 20 years in one hell-hole after another, he died, after being attacked and bitten on most of his body by a maniac, housed there with helpless, innocent souls unable to defend themselves.

Jerome is buried in the same cemetery as my mother and father: in hard clay soil, in an old, Long Island potato field. He was the Jesus of our family, who died for my sins.

29

MY FIRST AUTOPSY

[*from the radio*] "... to deep right field, that ball is going, going—
it is gone! Marris, hitting his second homer of the day and the Yankees'
sixth homer—"

And there is the nostalgic setup: the Mel Allen voice, one of the greatest voices radio has ever heard and one of the earliest radio voices that I came to love. Here I am, sitting in front of a microphone with a radio voice that millions love, and I'm going to tell the story of "My First Autopsy."

I was a late teenager, and I had gone on a big trip to Europe. You know, hippie, beatin' a trip to Europe; see the museums . . . blah, blah, blah. Came back on a ship, the Maasdam. Back from Europe and I felt a little off base—it was a kind of a little angst, a little nuts. So, I took a job at a mortuary, at Queens General Hospital. I can remember it to this day—red brick, big smoke stack, looked like a crematorium. I go in there as an assistant to just basically mop up and sweep up. I had never seen an embalming. I don't know why I took *that* job of all jobs: it was a bizarre choice to begin with. I guess it proves I was a little off base after going to Europe, but then again, I wouldn't be the first or last person to come back from Europe and think they were a little crazy—just take a look at Europe!

So, I go down into the morgue and I'm handed an apron and a mop. I'm told, "Basically, your job is to mop up the floor." Meanwhile, I'm watching the autopsies. This was my first autopsy. So, I watch the doctor. Now, here's a doctor with a medical degree; he was a medical examiner, performing an autopsy. He has a cigar in his mouth, which I thought was weird and kind of disrespectful to the dead. The guy is chomping on a cigar, he cuts open the dead woman's head, prying back the top of her skull to remove the brains for examination.

I'll never forget it as long as I live! She happened to be an African-American lady, and a large woman—and, he was pulling and pulling and pulling and the skull wouldn't pull off! So he puts his foot up against the stainless steel table and is pulling and cursing, and the cigar's ashes are falling on the corpse—and I'm the kid in the room there. I couldn't believe what I was watching! And, finally, he curses and the skull cap lifted off and that was it!

Then, I saw another corpse: the man must have been 50, 55; white man in good shape; slim; grey haired, but not old looking. Dead. And he was completely naked, as you'd expect on a slab. I'm mopping, mopping, mopping, and I look very carefully at the corpse. I notice some semen on his thigh, which was novel and unique because I didn't understand much about death at that time, as much as I've since learned.

And then there was a young child: two or three years old; as beautiful as a doll; blonde hair, blue eyes—like a doll. Still and dead, for no reason. Still and dead for no reason! I quit the next day and threw in my mop—and that was my first and last autopsy.

30

FIRST DEAD BODY

I remember those Cadillac hearses and a certain undertaker who showed me my first corpse in the morgue: hot day, July, Coca-Cola, ice box, outside, grocery story—now they call them bodegas, then they became clubs; you fished in the bottom of the Coca-Cola box; they had ice in it that turned to water and your arm turned blue as you fished around for a soda—that kind of day. And, the undertaker was there. My father was busy working in the back of his little shop, making a lamp or cleaning. He wired a lot of statues into lamps, and he was busy doing that. Broiling, hot day—I was outside, so I asked the undertaker what was going on in the mortuary.

He said, "Well, would you like to see what goes on?"

I said, "OK, sure." So, I get in the elevator—it was one of those loft-type elevators, where you pull a big cord from the top, an elevator from *The Godfather* that they moved cars on. To this day, I can hear the hum of that elevator: *mmmm*, the motor. I'm going down this huge car elevator into the basement, the subterranean depths of a funeral parlor. We get down there, walk, walk into the depths, and suddenly I witness an old woman being embalmed. She's all in pieces. Later, I came back up to the street—must have been a half hour later. My father is in an undershirt, outside the store, looking for me.

"Hey, Michael, where were you?" And when his eyes caught my eyes, he saw I was a changed person. And that's my undertaker story.

31

FIRST MORTGAGE

You know, I really hated 2007. Why must I love every year? Is that a liberal thing, that all years are equal—a moral equivalence between years? 2007 was a rotten year for me. What's the worst year of my life so far? I never thought about it that way. What's the best year of my life so far? Boy, I want to go back to my childhood. That's it. I want to live in the past. Walking around with a transistor radio; crew cut haircut; a little kid with corduroy pants; innocent; no sexual feelings—all that was on my head was baseball. But now, it's a different story: "What are you going to do? What are you going to do?"

There are so many problems. Who asked for this? I should disappear into the ether: white hat; West Palm Beach; Jupiter—maybe I should go to the planet Jupiter instead of Jupiter, Florida! You know that most of America walks around like they don't even know what's going on. They don't know where Iran is, for example! If you said, "Iran, Ahmadinejad, Hitler," they wouldn't know if you were talking about a baseball team or science fiction. They go to malls. All they want to do is jingle bells. Can you blame them? It's the way most people are.

So, why can't I be like most people? Answer: because I never was. I've always had the weight of the world on my shoulders. Even when I was a little kid in the Bronx they said, "That one has the weight of the world on his shoulders." They always said, "That one."

[*Savage to Producer*] Can you play "See the USA in a Chevrolet" with Donna Reed? I want to hear, "See the USA." [*plays music*] That's when there was still a Chevrolet; that was another time. It's like the Gillette Friday Night Fights: everything was different. It was a different world.

So, 2007 wasn't too great for me. I wouldn't say "horrible," OK? "Horrible" is death. Horrible is a family member dying. Horrible is a dog getting run over by your own car in the driveway. Horrible is the doctor saying you have bowel cancer and six months to live. Horrible is an emergency room. So, I'm not complaining—don't get me wrong—but I am, in my own way.

Remember this story? Bush comes up with a mortgage plan that will freeze certain sub-prime interest rates for five years. Now, in the face of it, you say, "Wow. How compassionate: a three-prong solution to stem the flow of mortgage foreclosures!" Now, let me ask you something: how many of these who were about to go into foreclosure are illegal aliens? Has anyone asked that question but me? Answer: no. The government, as you well know, was forcing banks to lend to people who were not only illegal aliens but also unqualified for a mortgage, and if the banks didn't lend the money to people who didn't qualify, they were going to be sued by various divisions of the US government.

Now the banks were about to go belly-up, and who was going to bail them out? The very same government that said, "You must lend money to them." Now, who's gonna pay for the bail out? You and I! *You and I!* Now, what about stronger lending standards? When I was young and I wanted to get a mortgage, I couldn't afford one—they wouldn't give me one. Why? Because I didn't qualify. Why couldn't I qualify? I didn't have sufficient income, therefore, I couldn't buy a house.

But you see, everything's changed in the new politically correct America. So, you have a socialist-lite government that said to banks for years, "You lend money to illegal aliens and unqualified minorities, or we will sue you." In fact, you can't even ask the so-called "citizenship status" of a potential borrower or, "We'll sue you for racism." So, the banks were over a barrel. They said, "But, but, but . . ." and the government said, "We'll give it to you in the you-know-what unless you lend it to the illegal alien and unless you lend it to people who don't qualify!" And now we have a so-called sub-prime crisis. So, Michael Savage again asks the question no one is going to ask: how many of these people in a sub-prime mortgage crisis are illegal aliens? How many of these people are those that banks were forced to lend to? But it doesn't stop Bush from telling us that we have to pay for it. Listen:

[*Bush*]: "Some lenders made loans that borrowers did not understand, especially in the sub-prime sector."

Whoa. Hold on. "Some lenders made loans that borrowers did not understand?" Is the President fooling you? What's there not to understand? Now he's taking the side of the people who they were forced to lend money to! You see why I said 2007 was a very bad year.

The first mortgage I ever heard about was the one my father secured in 1954 or 1955. He bought a house for $14,500 in Queens, New York. You had to put down 20 or 25 percent at the very least in those days. So, what would you have to put down then, about $3,000? It was a lot of money in those days. And then he took out a mortgage, and then he paid off the house. He had to qualify for the mortgage, and if he couldn't qualify, they wouldn't give it to him. And he paid off the house and that was the end of it.

In those days, my father wouldn't buy a car on time because he said that was cheating. Can you imagine how those old-timers thought? A mortgage you had to pay off, because who had cash to pay a whole house off? Nobody! Nobody did unless you worked for some people on a certain street that you ate spaghetti on, but the fact is, nobody that we knew had that kind of cash hidden behind the wallpaper in Bellerose, Queens.

So you had to take a mortgage, but a car was another story: you bought a used car and you paid cash. Why? Because if you bought it on time you were cheating; because you couldn't really afford it and you were a faker. By that thinking, 99.9 percent of the people on the road today wouldn't have a car.

32

KILLING MICE
IN A LABORATORY

When I first went to graduate school I was told to kill lab mice, as part of my duties. I refused. The professor warned me that I would lose my fellowship if I would not comply. He knew I had no other income except that $300 monthly stipend. I refused anyway; he dismissed me. I was always a purist and always paid for it. Here is that story.

The first year in graduate school I was in pharmacology. My job was to clean cages of mice. I'll never forget it as long as I live. I went into pharmacology: it was the first day. The professor—he was an evil doctor—said to me, "Your job is to pith the mice. Kill them." First, I had to clean the crap out of the cage. I remember hearing my deceased ancestors' voices saying to me, "This is what we evolved for, so that you could be cleaning up the droppings of a rodent?" I heard this in my head. It was as though my ancestors were talking to me.

See, I have a very unique relationship with my ancestors: they're all alive in my head when I want them to be—which is what makes me such a deep person, by the way. Many people are afraid of these things. They think they're schizophrenic or they've got to suppress it with drugs. Trust me, if you'll learn to be a "tap into your ancestry and talk to them when you want to and tune them out when you want to" kind of person, you could become an amazing human being.

So, I'm cleaning the cage and I hear (I don't know if it was my deceased father—actually it couldn't have been because he was still living, so it had to be another ancestor I never met) this voice.

"This is what we evolved for? Millions of years of evolution so you could stick your hand into a cage and clean up mouse droppings?" said the voice.

So, I thought back and replied to the voice, *Why? You're going to pay my rent? I mean, who's going to pay my rent?* I was making $300 a month in a fellowship at the time!

So that shut up the voice pretty well because I had to make a buck and that's what I had to do. I didn't mind cleaning the crap. I hated it, but I had to do it.

A few days later, this evil professor says to me, "Your job is also to pith—kill the animals, in other words. And he had a midget working for him—I'll never forget it as long as I live!—a midget woman who was a sadistic woman. She was frightening because she smiled while she did it. She said, "Michael, here's how you do it. You hold the mouse gently in your hand and make sure its head is between your thumb and forefinger so it can't move. You insert the thing here until you hear it pop, and it's dead."

So now I had a real conscience thing. I said, "I'm not killing these animals. I won't do it." So, I went to the professor and said, "Professor, I can't do this. I'm not going to kill these animals."

He said to me, "You have no choice. Either you kill the animals, or I'm canceling your fellowship and you're out of graduate school." He knew I was far away from home—I had no money. He was a real SOB, a real evil guy.

So I said, "Well, you'll have to do what you have to do." And he fired me. Threw me out of the laboratory because I wouldn't kill mice. And I wouldn't do it.

So, what could I do? I didn't put my tail between my legs. I was 6,000 miles away from home, so I said, "How can I stay in graduate school and not kill poor, little, innocent animals?" I went over to the botany department and talked to the head of the department and got a fellowship in botany. That's actually how I got into botany, believe it or not. Would you believe it? You talk about faith! Sometimes you've got to follow the river inside your own soul—I've got to tell you that—and not worry about it. If you really follow that strong river inside your soul, you're going to wind up on top 99 percent of the time. It's a great story. And it's 100 percent true.

So, it doesn't make me an animal rights wacko, although I'm not afraid to be called *that* amongst other things. I eat animals, truthfully, as I've told you. I don't enjoy the slaughter of animals; I don't hunt animals, although I don't condemn those who do. I didn't grow up hunting. We didn't hunt animals in the Bronx. If you grew up doing it, God bless you—it makes you a good soldier and a good

American. I didn't. It's just a different culture. I know how to use a gun, but I never envisioned shooting varmints with it.

Who did I have in my mind when I was shooting targets? Do you know that there was a rifle team in my high school when I was a youth? At Jamaica High School in Queens, we had a rifle team. Nobody picked up a gun and ran through the halls shooting anybody. Why? A) There was no psychotic medication; there was no Prozac, there was no Ritalin. Nobody was crazy. At that point, in America at that time, if you were crazy you weren't in high school. You were already filtered out earlier on. By the fourth, fifth grade they knew if you were a nut and they put you into a nut house or something—I don't know. But you didn't get into high school: they filtered you out. They didn't ask questions. They said, "Who's that nut over there in the second row? What's he doing there reaching inside his trousers in the middle of geometry class? Get him out of here!" They'd call the marshals and throw the kid out, or whatever. They didn't ask permission from some whack-job psychotic criminal, you know, with a medical history whether they could throw him out. They threw him out. B) The lawyers were not out of control in those days, either.

But to get back to the story: we had Mossberg .22 target rifles. To this day I can remember being in the basement of that school. Remember now, we're talking New York City, rifle team. I could smell the gunpowder. To this day I can hear the shots being fired. I would come up from that rifle experience: my head was clearer and I was able to focus better on school because I wasn't bored any more. The report of the rifle, the smell of the gunpowder, the camaraderie, and—more importantly—the men who taught us riflery were all World War II or Korean War veterans. Every one of them. That's who was teaching in those days. Compare it to today. To the marvins that they get, who tell you it's OK if you feel like putting on your mother's wig.

33

YOU DON'T KNOW
WHAT TOMORROW BRINGS:
White Males Need Not Apply

This is "The Savage Nation." It's been a long, long day's journey into night. If anyone knows what tomorrow's gonna bring, let me know about it. Send me a telegram. You don't know what tonight's gonna bring, let alone tomorrow. I mean, we make plans—sure, we plan. Everyone thinks they're going to live to a ripe old age. They're going to get a little ill—not totally ill, not very badly ill, never cancer or heart attack; nothing like that. That happens to other people. They're just going to slowly slow down, and they're going to wind up sitting quietly in a resort somewhere, a resort like a retirement community. They'll be able to take care of themselves right to the end, and they'll be surrounded by loving friends and family and die in their sleep at approximately 99 years of age.

Maybe 1 out of 500 million might go that way—or 1 out of 300 million. I don't really have the numbers—but, it's not happening to you. More likely, it will be a horrendous, slow death, either from cancer or some other debilitating disease—or, even worse yet, Alzheimer's disease, where you're left for hours at a time in a nursing home in a corner, staring at a curtain, unable to move and not knowing who you are. An orderly will beat you about the head and neck slowly with something that hides the blunt trauma and then steal the small change that your relatives bring you.

So, given that that's the fact of reality here and that I'm in a "long day's journey into night" mood—I've been in one since I was about 16 years old. I'm not sad, I'm not agitated. I'm just affected by this because, you know, the grim reaper comes around and he gets closer and closer, and you see him circling, and you start saying, "Here we go again." So, what is it that you want to do with the rest of your life? You have to ask yourself this if you're a driven man, as I am. I've been driven all my life.

I'm no saint: don't get confused, thinking I'm trying to tell you I'm such a saint. I'm not Al Gore or Barry Obama, OK? I'm just like you. Maybe I'm a little luckier and maybe I'm a little more hardworking than some people, but I'm not different than the average intelligent person out there. In some ways I'm a genius, and in some ways I'm a big idiot—I understand all of that. That's the full human being. But, I have a gift: there's no question that I have a gift for radio. It's probably inherent, innate. Nobody taught me how to do radio—and look where I am after 15 years. I'm in the winner's circle, just where I knew I would be!

Now, I could spend the next few years just trying to get to be No. 1, in the No. 1 slot. I could do that if I wanted, and I could probably win. I could change my time slot and go right up against Rush, and I'm telling you, Rush wouldn't stand a chance. In one year, he wouldn't be No. 1—I'd be No. 1! But I don't have such a desire; it doesn't mean anything to me. It has no meaning to me whatsoever! I've always seen the big picture; I've always seen the longer picture. There's very little I want materially. I only want my health and the health of my children, to be honest with you.

But then I say, "What about my poor country? What good is all this health, what good is a reasonable success, if the have-nots are being brought in by the tens of millions and if the have-nots are being told by these evildoers in politics that they can take from those who have created this? There's nothing to work for! They'll take it all away from your inheritors! They will give it away to the bums who didn't work for it—and that motivates millions of people like me.

Let me tell you right now: we don't want the illegitimate taking away our livelihood, and we don't want the illegitimate stealing any more of our damn tax money. Here in the state of California we pay 10 percent of our income as state income tax—10 percent right off the top! But wait, there's a bigger insult: a few years ago while you slept, they added another tax for people in a slightly higher bracket in the state of California—an additional 1 percent called a "mental health tax." So, that's 11 percent all together. Now what the heck is a mental health tax? Where does the money go? "Well," you say, "it goes for mental health." No, it probably goes to gray-bearded child molesters so they can write papers and go to conferences in Thailand and rape young boys—that's where the extra 1 percent goes! I can guarantee you it doesn't go into primary care.

And where will it end? Nobody knows where it will end. So, these are the things that are agitating me. People ask, "How long do we have?" The Athenian Republic did not last very long. In 1787 Alexander Tyler, a Scottish history professor, said, "A democracy is always temporary in nature; it simply cannot exist as a permanent form of government because a democracy will exist up until the time that voters discover they can vote themselves generous gifts from the public treasury." And that's the reason for the invented man called Obama—which allows him and his underlings to live like commissars in the ex-Soviet Union and tell you that they're "for the people." They are absolute Bolsheviks! They're right out of the Communist party, with a slight differential—and believe me, not a great differential at that.

Look at what happened with the Virginia Tech kids! These guys, these youngsters, were at the peak of their lives. They had their whole lives ahead of them—marriage and family—taken from them by an evil, sick bastard of the lowest order, who they're now glorifying as though he's the victim! That piece of scum, that scum who should never have been born, should have been buried with his head up in sand when he was born in Korea, as far as I'm concerned! They should have buried that boy when he was born, for the evil that he's done on this earth! That's how I see it. If you don't like it, sue me. Holding a separate memorial for him—can you believe it?—as if he is a victim of the system, too. You hear the psychosis of liberalism?

Let me pull back: I've seen a '57 Eldorado, in a garage in my neighborhood for a while now. I inquired of a neighbor's neighbor and went and looked at it yesterday. It was a '57 Eldorado, restored, framed up—a really nice car. I have a '65 Caddy convertible. I have a liking for '50s and '60s cars that are perfect. I don't really have the place to put it, but I looked at it. We talked, and this gentleman is from Sweden, a very nice man.

Before long we started talking about the Muslims' attempt to take over Sweden. I said, "How did you Vikings let this happen to you?"

He said, "We were too tolerant. They came in asking for asylum. We woke up and we can't go into some cities. Don't even get my mother started," he said. "My mother is vehement on this issue, that if we don't crack down on them and deport these imams, we're going to lose Sweden—" and on, and on, and on.

I said, "Well, look at the illegal aliens in America. Barack Obama is working around the clock to grant amnesty to 30 million illegal aliens, which will be the death of the United States of America as we know it. It will be over!"

As far as I'm concerned, it's a declaration of war against our sovereignty. Tens of millions of you understand what's at stake: you don't want the illegal aliens to be granted amnesty! You know what that will do to this country. You know it will give them the right to bring in five, ten, as many relatives as they want. Within five years you'll be living in Tijuana, with all of the horrors of Mexico on a street corner near you! Now if you want to live in Mexico, I suggest you go live in Mexico, but for God's sake, don't make this great nation into that corrupt socialistic dictatorship called Mexico!

34

WORKING THE SYSTEM

H ere's the connection to my awakening as a social worker: I learned that you shouldn't trust someone to deal honorably with you just because they smile when they speak your name. Sam the Butcher taught me that one. So, while I'd work with my clients, I could spot a phony a mile away. Here's when the scales started to drop from my eyes.

As a young social worker I made something like $5,500 a year. I was fresh out of college and had no furniture in my apartment. I had a mattress on the floor and orange crates for lamp tables, but I wasn't complaining: I had a job and it was a start. After all, as a child I had to manage with what we had, which wasn't much.

I'll never forget the day I visited one of the so-called welfare clients and what happened when I came back to my supervisor in the New York City Department of Social Welfare (or whatever it was called) to file my report. She wanted to know if they had furniture. When I said they didn't, she told me to take out a pen and paper.

She said, "Michael, write this down: they're setting up an apartment, Mr. and Mrs. Whomever. Every civilized family needs a bed—write down $350 for a bed. They need two lamp tables—write down $120 each. In the living room, they need a coffee table—write down $120. They'll need a sofa—write down $300."

This went on for a few minutes. The whole time I'm thinking about my empty apartment and how I could use all of those things, but not wanting to lose my job, I knew better than to speak up as my supervisor told me to have a check cut for $5,327.92, all so those welfare leeches could have a "decent home."

35

THE FINAL STRAW

The moment I decided to go to the top of the teaching profession, that's when I slammed into another ugly truth about liberalism that put me on another political course. I left teaching and went to graduate school, where I laboriously worked on two Master's degrees and then a Ph.D. from the University of California at Berkeley. Major-league publishers had published six or eight of my books by the time I graduated.

When it was time to get my teaching job, I was told, in effect, "White men need not apply." Keep in mind, I had a nearly perfect "A" average in my graduate courses; my master's dissertation was published in a major scientific journal (the *Journal of Ethnobotany* from Harvard); my Ph.D. was published as a book! This combination would have automatically ushered me into the halls of academia in any other past generation. That's when the worm turned; that's when I became radicalized; that's when I saw the true color of liberalism! Here I had two young children and I had killed myself to get that degree, but because of the social engineering of the radical Left, I was told to put aside all of my aspirations.

Affirmative action, a misguided liberal policy supposedly used to promote equal opportunity, almost destroyed my family and I. Here I was a "man-child in the Promised Land," denied my birthright for matters of race. According to the ACLU this immigrant son had "to put his life on hold" so the less-qualified (i.e. "others") could move ahead. The rest is history.

I will not bore you with the details or whine. I do very well indeed today, but the government didn't hand it to me. Welfare didn't get me to where I am today! It's been a long road of crawling on broken glass. Everything I ever achieved

I achieved with hard work, dedication, sweat, tears, and pain. By the way, none of those qualities are taught today. I guess you could say I'm a fighter; I do not now, nor have I ever, expected someone to hand me an entitlement, especially not the government.

I fight and work for what I want in life—always have.

36

WORKING ON CRUISE LINES

Have I told you about the Force Ten storm? Let me tell you. It's a true story.

This was one of the most frightening moments of my life because my family was on the ship. When I was a younger guy, when I was on the islands as an anthropologist and ethno-botanist, I took great slides with my Nikon F, in the light meter days. Those were the days of real photography. I'm not saying you can't do it with digital: you can, because I have a digital camera, and I'm very fond of it. I really don't know how to compare the two. I'm very happy with the digital pictures, but the day of holding the light meter and stepping back—that was another story. Hearing the shutter click on a Nikon F was visceral photography. Those were exciting days of taking pictures! You took slides in those days.

Does anyone do slides anymore? I don't think so. I don't think anyone does a slide, but the quality of the depth of the picture was phenomenal. I have some pictures, for example, of kids—and these were mixed-race kids, incidentally—in the Cook Islands, circa 1970 or 1971, laughing on a roadside as I went by. I started to talk to them, right after a light rainstorm.

Because I had great slides, I approached the cruise lines about presenting slide shows of the islands the ships traveled. I was always in love with big ships. As a kid in Queens, New York, where I was landlocked, I grew up in a family that didn't know boating from a lox. I used to drive on the West Side Highway when I first got my car in New York. The great cruise ships of the world would line up on the Hudson River piers, and I would drive by. They were the most beautiful visions I'd ever seen! Each ship was filled with the promise of a thousand lifetimes to me. I don't know what drew me to the sea in that way, but I said to myself that when

I got older, whatever I did, that I'd have to go to sea in some way or another. Now, I didn't go into the Navy—fate did not take me there. Perhaps that would have been another life and a great life unto itself, but, as I say, I went to the Islands and took these great pictures. Then, as I had children but still wanted to get out there and didn't have the money to do so, I marketed myself in a proper manner. I went to the cruise lines and said, "I can lecture your passengers about the Islands," which was true.

So, I got a free first-class cabin for my wife and I, and another one for the kids. I took the kids out of school often, and I'd get the question, "Should you take your kids out of school for a month at a time? They'd fall behind in lessons."

I remember saying, "Look, son, I'm taking you out of school for a month. This is a great privilege to go on a ship. You're going to have to take your lessons with you. We're going to do the lessons on the ship, and you're going to keep a journal."

"Sure, Dad."

Needless to say, three days out and the journal was still blank. The pages were blank; the schoolbooks were still sitting on the shelf. The kids were wheeling around on the deck on the ship, bothering all the old people who hated children. They were the only children on the ship, in some cases, because who else had a child on a ship in those days in the month of, let's say, October or November? Nobody.

So, one of the ships we got on was not a big ocean liner. It was small: 5,000 tons with a very shallow draft that let it into shallow waters, as in the Antarctic. So my family and I went back and forth between Tahiti and Fiji in two cabins. The ship didn't have many passengers. Remember, for the average cruise ship then, a big ship was 35,000 tons. Today, they're 100,000 tons or 125,000—They're monsters! They're hotels with propellers! I don't particularly like monster ships.

So, I'm on a 5,000-ton boat with a very shallow keel. We leave Fiji, and we're supposed to be out there, back and forth, for about 20 days, island-hopping to Tahiti around Christmastime or New Year's. Well, we got into a hurricane. Now, you got a light, shallow-bottom ship in a storm, and this ship is rolling. In the middle of the night I heard a pounding. They put us toward the bow of the ship, in forward cabins: not exactly the best. I hear banging like someone's hitting the steel hull with a sledgehammer, so I wake up and say, "Something is wrong. Why is the ship sounding like this?" I get up, go in the passageways: nobody is awake.

Being a survival type, I knew something was wrong. I threw on a windbreaker, climb up to the bridge, and there is the German captain, who is normally as nattily dressed as you would expect of a sea captain. Now he is unshaven, in an undershirt, and his eyes are in another state. They weren't in a state of panic, but they were locked: locked onto another place in another time, and he looks at me as though I'm not there—he looks right through me! His hands were locked on the wheel. It wasn't a state of panic, but his eyes were looking somewhere away— maybe, you would say, like a soldier when they say "1,000 yard stare". That's what he had, the 1,000 yard stare.

He had gone a little nuts from the pressure. He said, "Lecturer, all the time Fiji, Tahiti; Tahiti, Fiji. Lecturer, Fiji, Tahiti; Tahiti, Fiji." He had reached the breaking point. We were in a terrible storm, and it was very rough, very bad. I feared the ship would go down. After this experience, I became kind of disinterested in taking my children on long trips on small ships.

Now, I would ask you, if you came from a family that took you away on long trips as a child, did it affect you positively in the long run, or negatively? Here's the interesting twist to this whole story: it was actually liberal thinking in those days that, if you took your child out of school for a long trip and they were exposed to the world, they would get more out of that long exposure than they would from sitting in a classroom. That was actually a liberal philosophy, which I went along with and ascribed to—and it turned out to be correct!

FIRST BOAT IN HAWAII:
Sailing for First Time

One day we were playing Hawaiian music on the show and it reminded me of the days when I lived there for a number of years. Imagine what it's like for a kid from New York to wind up in Hawaii: I'd never been to a place like that! It was like walking into heaven itself, or so I thought as I picked fallen plumeria blossoms from the sidewalks.

When you land in heaven you think you can do anything. You are filled with a sense of confidence that only children and the mad have and can understand. But, when a grown-up has hubris, it becomes very dangerous and, in my case, that was true. I had never seen sunsets like in Hawaii. I used to bicycle up to the university, and I would see plumeria blossoms lying on the sidewalk. I would stop the bicycle and pick up the blossoms and look at them and smell them. Sure, I had seen roses on a fence in the Bronx when I was a little kid and they were soft and beautiful, but this was something unique. The sweet scent was unlike anything I had ever experienced.

Sunsets and sunrises and birds in the jungles in the back of the rainforest, that you'd never seen or heard before—and you started to get tuned into your own body in a way you'd never been. If you've never lived in the tropics and it's the first time, you start shedding clothing and shoes and leather, and you put it all away. And now you're in flip-flops and shorts. All of a sudden at night the breeze blows gently through your sleeves and you start to come alive in a new way. You go in the warm water and start to feel like the original man. So you buy a sailboat—that's the first thing you do.

So, I bought a sloop-rigged boat. "Tarange" was a sloop-rigged sailing vessel, about 22 feet long. She was made of white oak primarily and was built in Oregon, then sailed out to Hawaii. I bought her for next to nothing. She was in perfect shape and had no engine. I berthed her in the Ala Wai Yacht Harbor. Most people who own boats mainly use them to drink on and hang out—it's as good a thing to do as any—but I was foolish enough to actually want to sail the boat, even though I knew nothing about sailing. I took it out without an engine.

I knew it was pretty easy to get out because the wind was prevailing out of the yacht harbor. I thought, *Wow, this is great!* There I was on the boat alone. My friends cast me off, released the lines, pushed me backwards, and there I went: down the Ala Wai Channel, out of the harbor, out into the ocean. I was zipping along with the sail all the way out.

And there I was out in the Pacific Ocean, alone. *This is super. I'm really enjoying myself.* Then I realized I didn't know how to get back. I thought, *How do I turn this thing around if the wind is blowing out?* Well, I didn't know how, so I thought, *Well, I better figure this out because if this keeps up for a while, I'll soon be out in the middle of the ocean—and then there will be no way back at all.*

I had no flares, no radio, no engine. All I had was confidence that was bordering on the insane. The first thing I did was resort to common sense. I dropped the sails because that would cut the motion of the boat. I dropped the sails and, using the tiller, turned the boat around—you know: flip flop, flip flop—until I got the boat pointing back towards the land. Then, I figured, *If the wind is blowing against me, there must be way to go into a prevailing wind and still move against it. I've seen other people do it.* And little by little, lo and behold, I was able to— luckily (I don't know whether it was the current or God's hand itself)—get pushed back into the harbor. I learned quickly that sailing is not for the amateur. That's all there is to it.

Those days are over, but she was my first boat. I didn't save the life ring from "Tarange" because I didn't even have a life ring. I don't think I even had a life preserver! That was in the late '60s, an age when people thought with total madness about what they could do and accomplish.

Now I drive a powerboat. It has all sorts of safety equipment on it, but not as much as it should have. But, I like powerboats a lot better than sailboats because they're easier to get out. I can get this boat underway in 15 minutes. It's 45 feet long, twin diesels, 19 tons, and I can go out on it alone and come back on it alone in almost any wind. That's the good part: just you and the birds and the water, the wind and the land. That's why I go out now, just to look at the water and look at the birds and look at the landforms, mainly—and the seals. I can name every species of bird on the Bay. I've come to understand that every animal has a personality—isn't it strange?

I still eat animals, but they all have a personality when you get to know them—and they all want to live. Dad taught me that everything wants to live. That's how he taught me to respect human life. He said, "You'll notice that a cat wants to live, a dog wants to live, a rat wants to live, a mouse wants to live, a bird wants to live." He learned that when he accidentally shot a bird as a kid. Remember, this is odd to a country boy—it sounds very weak, but remember, I'm a New York City boy. To us, it's a different experience than it is to you guys. I respect your ability to hunt for your food—but every animal actually has a personality when you get to know it. They're all different, just as we're all different: every human is unique, like a snowflake. Well, guess what? So are animals! They're all unique. It's amazing when you come to understand that.

38

FIJI ISLANDS IN 1969, AND HOW FIJIANS WERE UNIQUE

When I first arrived as a plant collector in the Fiji Islands in 1969, these Islands in the South Pacific were still a colony of Britain. They received their independence the next year. It was strange to me, so I asked many people why, after colonialism, Fiji was a fairly stable nation without much violence and why the people were generally not hostile towards whites.

Here's what people told me: I don't know whether there's any veracity to this, but the folks I met down there said to me that the British were generally monstrous in their treatment of colonial subjects around the world. The joke in Fiji was that they needed one place to go when they retired—and that place was going to be Fiji, so they decided to treat Fijians better than they treated other subjects in other places. As a result, the Fijians were not anti-white. I don't know if there's any truth to that.

When I first arrived in the Islands, I wound up in a riverbed on the Waindina River as the only white boy surrounded by black men who were pretty huge—pretty large and pretty muscular. I was prepared for the worst because of my own biases from where I came from, but frankly, they turned out to be some of the kindest people in the world; took me into their villages, and we drank a lot of kava kava for many a night. What I learned years later is that the Fijian people are an exception to all rules, not just with regard to post-Colonialism!

The Fijians are a unique breed of people to begin with. It has nothing to do with race. It has everything to do with something else, and nobody knows what that is.

39

ARE WE ALL DEAD?

I once told a story about when I was in Fiji very late at night, after drinking kava kava all night. I was in a village, I don't know, three or four miles away from the home village where I was staying on the plant collecting trip. For some reason I did not want to stay in the village I was visiting that night. I just didn't want to stay there—I don't know what it was! It was the middle of the night, and I was compelled to walk back to the other village. Now my guide didn't want to go with me. He said, "Michael, are you sure you want to go at night?"

I said, "Yes, I've got to get out of here."

I haven't any idea why. I left on my own; I said I'd find my way back. Well, I walked back along the edge, on a trail—it was on the edge of a bluff. I knew the ocean was below. It was crashing below me, and I could hear that. I could vaguely see that. It was a dark night, not even a moonlit night, but I followed the footpath. I got back safely.

The next morning my guide showed up and said to me, "Do you have any idea what you walked on?"

I said, "No."

"Come back with me."

So we went back on the path. In some places the path had less than two inches of soil to the right of the path. I could have fallen a couple hundred feet to my death into the dark sea below the cliff-side trail—but I didn't! How do you explain that? I didn't see the path; I kind of felt my way in the dark. That's not a religious or supernatural experience, on one hand. On the other hand, could you say that an angel was guiding my feet?

How about the time a car hit me when I was a young boy and I bounced halfway across the street. I walked out from between two parked cars in Jamaica, Queens and got banged in the air. I don't know, why didn't I get killed? Why did it just graze me? Why did the driver stop and say, "Are you OK?"

Or, did I get killed and die, and is this all a dream? Did you ever have one of those? Maybe I'm dead. Maybe you're dead and imagining you're reading this . . . .

40

HARRY THE UNDERTAKER
and SIDNEY DYING OF CANCER

Life has been good to me. "I've had my share," as Harry the Undertaker once said to me. Did I ever tell you about Harry the Undertaker? (I hope his family is not listening). I told you about Sidney, didn't I? Sidney, the old man who was dying of cancer years later? I'll tell you about him, then Harry the Undertaker. As he was dying and in severe pain, the girls would go by in the market. He was moaning. He still wore a neat little suit, though—tie, jacket—and the slits that were his eyes would light up when he saw a pretty girl. As the girls walked by he'd say, "Oh, Mikey!" A pretty girl would walk by and he'd say—

(Now I've got to put this in a family way and change it a bit because I grew up around men who spoke a little on the vulgar side. Even though I was a kid, they didn't check a dictionary).

So anyway, he'd say to me, "I would like to make love to her once more," as the woman went by.

I said, "You made love to her? This strange, beautiful woman?"

He said, "No, Mikey, once more I'd like to make love to her." He turned the words around.

Although he was poor, he considered himself a ladies' man. He wore cologne. He wore a suit. He reminds me of that other old gentleman: Harry the Undertaker, a dapper little fellow who chauffeured the funeral cars, lived next door. Years after my conversation with Sidney, when I was 14, I asked Harry about women:

I said, "Do you monkey around?"—or something like that.

He said, "No, Mikey. I had my share."

That was dignified. That a man would say, "I had my share," was an amazing thing for me to hear, because most guys pretend that they're in heat 24/7. They're ready to rut like a rooster in a barnyard and every woman is fair game, they say. You know, that's how guys put on the act.

In reality, most men really aren't like that. It's very unnatural to be in heat 24/7. But this guy was dignified. He said, "No, Mikey. I had my share." That was the most dignified thing a man ever said to me.

41

THE LEATHER MAN
GETS BRAIN CANCER

This is about a man who grew up as one of my father's best friends in a very poor neighborhood in New York City. They were immigrants together; their parents came over, maybe on the same boat, or they met each other in the slums of New York. They both had a very tough life, and they worked their way up, little by little, as the immigrants have to do as they struggle in any society. This man went into a business that took off at a certain point like a rocket: he hit a fad in a certain business and started to make a great deal of money. He moved way beyond our family.

While we lived in an attached brick house in Queens, he had the money to move his family to a detached house. I remember how important that distinction was in those days: it's like the Buick LeSabre as opposed to the Buick Roadmaster—or, God forbid, you were Rockefeller and bought a Cadillac, if you can imagine. People used to grade their status in those days by their car model and house. I don't suppose it's much different today: it just isn't as easy to figure out in some regard—not on the road anyway.

So he moved to this detached house in Roslyn, New York. It was a beautiful house. It had its own lawn all around it (we only had a little strip of grass in the backyard and a tiny one in the front). The carpet was wall-to-wall and pink.

He was a big cigar smoker. We would go and visit; I had a very good time. He would gloat with the cigar and lord it over my father. We'd leave. My father never said anything against him, but you know, I could see in his eyes that he was a little, let's say, that he lost that little battle at that time. You know how humans are: they're competitive! Even if they love their friend, if their friend does better than them, there's a degree of envy in every human being. It's just one of the cardinal sins.

As years went on, the man's business continued to thrive. Then I left home and moved away from NYC. I went and did my thing collecting plants, working for my graduate degrees thousands of miles away—I was living 6,000 miles away, then 9,000 in the Fiji Islands. Lo and behold, on one of my trips back to New York, when I was already a father myself, I heard that this man's leather business had collapsed entirely. The fad that he rode like a wave died. People were no longer buying that particular product, and the man who had a chain of successful wholesale stores lost everything.

He lost everything, and it was so fast that he wound up living where he started: on the Lower East Side of New York in a poor relative's apartment, with his wife and the relative's family—back where he started in a one-room apartment. And that's where I come in.

I came back from one of my trips to the Fiji Islands. I was a young man— I don't remember how old I was; maybe 35 to 40. My father was dead, and here sits the leather man. Now, remember, I loved him like another father. I loved all my father's friends. You know how it is when you're a kid in a very close-knit community: you tend to love the people like they're your own. We all grew up so close together, and there was never a bad word between him and my father.

He sat there, shrunken up in the chair in my parents' living room, after he'd lost everything. He looked up at me, still smoking a cigar, and practically pleaded, "Michael, Michael, look what happened to me. Look what happened to me." His eyes were wandering left and right. He didn't understand what happened to him. He said, "I'd rather have cancer than what God did to me."

Lo and behold, I soon left New York again. I went back to do what I did, which was collect plants, and I heard that two years later he died from one of the most rapidly invasive forms of brain cancer.

Be careful what you say: God hears the truth but waits.

42

FROM IMMIGRANT'S SON TO RADIO STARDOM

My father was an immigrant. He came here when he was 13. He was not born here, but I was born here. He was a citizen when I was born. I'm not an anchor baby—don't get me wrong—but I do have one foot in the Old World and one foot in the New World, so I really speak from a knowledgeable position about it. I understand what it's like to live in a poor household with many people. Trust me, we lived in such a place—we didn't even have a bedroom in the Bronx. Now that I think about it, there was one bedroom and a tiny living room with a fake fireplace. I remember hanging stockings on the fake fireplace: I thought Santa would give me a gift.

So, part in the Old World, part in the New World. My grandmother didn't speak a word of English in the house. She spoke the old language from the old country. She was so wonderful! Boy, did I love her. She was so beautiful; very stoic; very, very Russian, this woman. She spoke to me in Russian by the way. I am not a Russian language speaker, but it's strange: I can understand the language to a certain extent. It's a very hard language for an American to learn incidentally. It's not an easy language! The alphabet is very complicated for an English speaker. I can surely imagine how hard it is for a Spanish-speaker to learn English, by the way. English is a tough language, very tough!

But, in my home, my parents spoke only English. To make a long story short, here I am, a "man-child in the Promised Land." When my turn came to assume my position in this country in my chosen profession, they said, "White men need not apply." The positions were closed. So, you can understand where I am coming from. I got so angry that I produced a virgin demo in 1993 and sent it out to about 220 radio stations. I got a return from about five to ten of them. Five of them said, "That's really good stuff. Would you like to work at our station?" I remember, to this day: one of them was in Boston of all places. I don't remember the stations that said, "We like what you did," but, nevertheless, I was living in San Francisco as I am now and one of the offers came from a local station. The guy said to me, "Good stuff. Would you like to come on in and talk to us?"

I did an anniversary show a few years ago and retold this story to celebrate the occasion. Here's what the virgin demo said, from 1993, which I played during that show:

"And now, direct from the towers above Manhattan, it's "The Michael Savage Show." To the right of Rush and to the left of God, and now—Michael Savage."

"I'm glad I can be with you seven nights a week because these stories are just not going away. I mean, every day in every way we're getting assaulted. Look at these questions before us today. Look at the questions before us! You know they say that I'm to the right of Rush and to the left of God: I really don't think that's funny. I really don't think that's funny at all! Do immigrants carry diseases? Are lawyers really humans?"

Alright, let's pause. You see how daring this was? You say, "Well, it's commonplace today," but it was not commonplace in 1994, it was really daring. It broke open new ground. I changed the media landscape! That's it; that's how I started.

Then I did a show—I'll never forget it. I blew through it because I was under the weather. I'll never forget it: the local station manager called me and said, "Would you like to fill in?"

I said, "Sure, I'll try it." Now, I had never done radio except on book tours. I had done 10 national book tours, where you go around and do radio and television. They were very stressful. Along the way I remember various program directors saying to me, "You know, you're really good on the radio. You should consider a career in radio." How could you get a job in radio? It was as real to me as becoming an astronaut. Of course I wanted to do it, but I didn't know how to get into radio.

But let me tell you something: desperation breeds creativity and creativity breeds a lot of opportunity. I think that fate had a hand in it; this, and God. I really think I was set out to do this from the beginning! Alright, so he says, "fill in." The first show I filled in for was on a liberal talk station in San Francisco—

it's still there. It's a powerhouse 50,000 watt-er. He gives me a show to fill in for. The guy is on the overnight show and is a hater of the lowest order, hates white people—let's say, like Obama's pastor. Exactly, a Reverend Wright! All night long, hate radio: against whites, against America. He himself, of course, is living the high life—as is Reverend Wright in his new $10 million house. You understand how it works. Curse America and laugh all the way to the bank, you know. All they needed was the Kool-Aid, like a Jim Jones' job.

So, that's the kind of show I filled in on! I never listened to the creep and I'm never up in the middle of the night. So, I go on the air and I start to tell about illegal immigrants. Soon the hate callers began. I was overwhelmed because remember what my last incarnation was? I was the good doctor, the nutritionist and the herbalist who gave lectures around the world! And by the way, I had even given a lecture—you'll never believe this story, I don't think I've told it.

Normally, I would give lectures about health and vitamins and nutrition in America. At one point, I was director of nutrition for a major international nutrition company. They sent me to Malaysia to talk about their products. My audience was all Muslim women, and they were a great audience. These were moderate Muslim women who were interested in nutritional supplements. They received it very well. I spoke and it was translated.

So, I had been all over the world doing lectures and I was usually very well received. Frankly, I was like the "beloved doctor"—that kind of thing. Now I do talk radio, and I walk into a propeller of hatred from the Left. I never encountered such hatred from the people, from the regular listeners of this guy's show! That night, when the shift ended, (I think it was from 1 to 5 a.m.) I drive home from that station. The whole way home I'm in a paranoid state. I'm looking in the rearview mirrors—I thought I was being followed! I get home. I say to my family when I get home, when they wake up, "I'm never going to do radio as long as I live. I can't take the hatred of the callers! The liberals are the most hateful people I've ever encountered in the world. No amount of money would be worth doing this!"

The station called me the next day when I woke up. They said, "Wow, you did a great job, Savage! Would you like to fill in again?"

I said, "No, I will never fill in again as long as I live. I don't ever want to do radio again." Ask them! I'm not making it up!

"Why?"

"I'm not going to go into a show again with these haters."

"Well, how about filling in during the day?"

I said, "I don't know. I don't think I could do radio: it's too hateful. The people who call are full of hate, the Left-wingers."

So they said, "Tell you what: you won't have to do the night shift again. You'll do a day shift."

I did a little fill-in on the day, and I shook up the whole local media. Then eventually they created a local conservative station and I went on that. They made me an offer I couldn't refuse. Remember, I was making a fairly good living as an author and consultant. I didn't want anything to do with radio, but the temptation was too great.

I've got to tell you something else. Radio—you ask anyone in the media who knows how to do it right and they'll all tell you the same thing—nothing in the world of media could compare to the high you get off radio. There's nothing that can compare to the feelings you get! When you do this right, there's no performance in the world that equals radio.

43

THE MEDICAL REASON
WHY LIBERALISM
IS A MENTAL DISORDER

I wrote the bestselling book *Liberalism is a Mental Disorder*. The title says it all. The only explanation for extreme liberalism is madness—in some cases, mild; in some cases, severe. How could they think these things unless they're crazy? Sometimes they're not totally crazy, just partly crazy, but they're crazy for the things that they do—why? I knew a medical doctor 20 years ago who was an early pioneer in acupuncture in America. He practiced in Sausalito on a houseboat. He was the nicest guy in the world. He was a good doctor who had studied in China, and he was a legitimate, straightforward American medical doctor. In the '70s he went to China and came back and incorporated acupuncture, and it worked so well that he gave up regular medicine and only practiced acupuncture.

According to acupuncture theory, there's a thing called a "sorter" that goes out in some people. I asked him, "What does that mean?" It's the ability to sort out what is relatively important and what is relatively unimportant in a person's life, he told me. In other words, it distorts. Their sorter is out, so in other words, the acupuncturist hits certain pressure points to make the sorters work again so that people can get things in order in their lives. That's so typical of people who are extremists: they're unable to sort things out in their minds as to what's important and what's unimportant, whether it be in their own lives or in the life of the society or in their place in society. Their sorters are off! That's a form of illness—whether you want to call it a mental illness is another story.

I will tell you, a lot of statements that come out of the liberal orthodoxy are examples of this distortion. Maybe what they need is a good needle in the right place.

44

THE DEATH OF PETS:
Snowy Story

My poor little dog, Snowy, is going to die. Now this is not Teddy, my current dog, but my last dog, Snowy the Border Collie. She's 16 years old. For years I called Snowy my little angel with fur. I even wrote a poem to her. Three years ago, if you remember, she became quite feeble. I couldn't take care of her. People said, "Well, euthanize her," but I said, "No, she's not ready for death." We found some good, kind folks up near the Russian River who took her in, and she's had three more beautiful years. She got better living on their little farm. She became the queen of the other dogs—they loved her! Well, she's gotten sick, very sick. So we went up to see her; took a long, silent ride. When we got there she was lying in the grass, and her eyes were glazed over. She was very thin. It was very sad.

What can I say to you? She was a big part of my life. I love the dog, but she didn't die. I whistled to her and talked to her and said, "Come on, let's go for a run." As she lay there, she tried to run, but her feet moved only slightly.

Snowy didn't die on Saturday. She just lay there breathing heavily, and then we took her in the house. I didn't know what to do with her, but she was very peaceful. When I left her in the house, the little place where she lives, I said, "You know, we should all be so lucky as to lie down in the grass in the cool shade, surrounded by people who love us, when it's the end of our lives." It's a part of the cycle of life.

45

WHEN PASTA WAS SPAGHETTI

I found "When Pasta was Spaghetti" in my archives. It was written—let's see—"Michael Savage, August 1985, written in a lightning storm at 40,000 feet over Cheyenne, Wyoming." When I thought the plane was going to crash, I wrote "When Pasta was Spaghetti." So, you liberals get ready to sneer, and you sane people get ready to enjoy it because it's a wonderful poem. So, play the music again. Go ahead: try to imagine it, alright?

"The hairy forearms of New York serve you your coffee with a turning gesture, an offering that says, "Drink, eat, enjoy." The wiry Italian in Vincent's Clam Bar, the one behind the greased-over register; the young kid connected, the one who receives his deference from the spaghetti cook, older than his gangster father—the spaghetti cook who looks like an old-fashioned doctor from the Bronx, with clipped mustache. He actually pulls some noodles out of the pot and eats them as they cook, looking to the grimy ceiling for his tender answer. Well, they used to call it "spaghetti." Now it's "pasta" at $10 a plate. The smoky windows of Romeo's Spaghetti now offer radios and knick-knacks. It was 50 cents a plate then. In neon letters that you couldn't miss, even through a fogged-over window on a cold winter's eve, there was life: marinara sauce that stuck to the seat; noodles as long as your young arm; meatballs as fluffy as your dreams of them; bread on the table that you'd eat against your parents' admonition that, "the meal was a-coming, the meal was coming." And men, some burly with black hairy forearms, whose smiles scared you. And little skinny guys with the look of murder on their faces, and people who slurped their spaghetti straight to their mouths from the plate, one motion like Chinese shoveling rice at mouth with clicking sticks. That was gusto before it became a beer ad. That was taste before it became a synonym for fashion. That was spaghetti before it became pasta."

Very good—I'll do that for private readings for $100,000 for my favorite charity. You want me at your party? I'll come and read, "When Pasta was Spaghetti." What if I actually had a gangster call me up: "Mike, we want you to come read 'When Pasta was Spaghetti,' and we'll give you 100 grand. It's nothing to us." I would do it. I read that an actor gets a million dollars per private performance. Can you believe this? The guy started as a street mime in San Francisco— unbelievable!

I was too good for anything. You ever go through that? That's why a lot of people wind up bums: they're too good to do anything so they end up doing nothing. They wind up living in their parents' house smoking dope, but they're "waiting to be discovered." Everyone's got to sell-out, just sell off for the highest price you can. That's the whole story.

46

REPUBLICANS SHOULD TREAT VOTERS LIKE CUSTOMERS IN RESTAURANTS

Let me ask you something: do you eat in chain restaurants? Does anyone eat in chain restaurants anymore? Some I like for the anonymity; young servers, very cheerful. The girls have four to five little earrings in their lobes, which means they're nymphos, but there's something about young people in a chain restaurant. They're so eager to please. They were probably molested as youth, but they serve well. You get the bread right away, the beer.

I ate in that chain, "Backout." I like it a lot, that Aussie chain. You know why? I'll tell you why I like it: no one knows me, which I love. The only thing I don't like is the lamp over the table. I feel like I'm in a '50s *Dragnet* movie, like, "Where were you on the night of the —?" You know, it blinds you! Who created that? I don't like a light in the top of my eyes when I'm trying to eat, but, if you order a 7 oz. steak, you get a 7 oz. steak—and where can you get a baked sweet potato in a restaurant?

I swilled beer; I sat there. There was one table with a crying child. I only moved twice—I only had to move twice. Look, in life you're going to hear a child screaming. Don't get me wrong. I don't hate children. I said to the nympho waitress, "Look, the kid's making noise. I'd like to move." They think you don't like kids. It's not like I don't like children! I said to them, "Look, I raised children. I love them, but I work very hard and when I come for dinner I can't listen to them." The girl waiters seem to understand better than the boy waiters, who don't even understand what I say.

I recently went to a Thai restaurant for lunch. I'm going to tell you about a dog and a shrimp because I have a rough thing with shrimp. It's on and off with me and shrimp: you especially can't trust them in the summer—and even in the winter! You know, the Jewish prohibitions against shrimp were not bad. The Muslims picked that up. They were smart. It's not a bad prohibition because shrimp are iffy. They're very iffy creatures—but I happen to like them.

Now, Teddy loves shrimp. He loves them if I cook them and I don't spice them, nothing on them. Then I cool it off in a glass of water and I give it to him. Loves it! Knocks it down! Now, listen to what happened: this is an important story. Ted is my "canary in a coal mine" when it comes to testing shrimp. I'm in a Thai restaurant for lunch. I'm itching—I had to put a lotion on my forearms after the lunch, which is not a good sign. I got a little itch on both forearms, which is the first sign of some contaminant, some taint. They let me sit on the outside deck with the dog, which is why I go there.

I ordered the "fisherman's dish." I didn't like the smell of the seafood. It was presented nicely, but right away there was a slight "off" smell. You know how with seafood you can smell it immediately if you have a good olfactory sense? But I ate it anyway. Here's the thing about me: why did I eat it anyway? Because A) I paid for it, B) I was hungry, and C) I figured *Alright, it wasn't that bad,* and I don't have enough willpower to send it back. I don't want to start in with the sending back.

Now, here's the trick: I eat all the shrimp, but he's looking. I said, "Teddy, I can't feed you. I told you that it's Thai food when we come here," and he knew it was too spicy, so he didn't even beg. Toward the end, though, he lost his composure and asked for something. I couldn't resist because he was a good boy, slept under the table, so what did I do? I dipped the shrimp in water and whatever was on it came off—and I gave it to him. You know what he did? He wouldn't eat it! But here's the funny part: he rolled on it. I'd never seen him do this! He would not eat the shrimp—he rejected it, probably because it was tainted and tricked up by the Thais in that restaurant—and here's the stranger part: he mashed it on his head, all over his fur! So, I reached down and said, "What are you doing? Why are you rolling in it?" He gives me a growl like he doesn't know me when I try to take his shrimp away!

The only thing I could figure out is that the shrimp gave off the scent of a female dog and he fell in love with it. He was trying to make love to a shrimp on the ground! He was mashing it all over his head, his ears, and his eyes, and it was all over his fur. I don't like when they give you the white-eye. When those little nice dogs all of a sudden give you a white eye, it can be frightening. They can rip your hand off! Normally, he's a nice boy. I said, "What, are you crazy? I gave you the shrimp. Why are you growling at me?" It was the crazy eyes. So, I mashed it aside, and then a fly ate it.

I must tell you, if there's another chain restaurant I could eat in, I'm going to go. No more of the, "Hey, Mike, how are you doing?" I don't need a free meal; I don't want a free meal. I don't need any friends in the restaurant business—they wind up treating a tourist off the street better than they do people they know, by the way. That is a peculiar thing, you know. Did you ever see that, "You're an old-time customer?" And, I'm a celebrity, to top it off, that talks about food! I don't mean they treat me badly, but they get a guy off the street who they never saw before and they cater to him more than people they know! What is *that* all about? What are you, a given? You're like someone they know, they own? So, this one new customer will build a new customer base? I don't know.

To me, you have to treat your customer base right. See, the Republicans ought to think of the nation as a restaurant. If the Republicans treated the American electorate as customers in a restaurant, they would win. But they can't do it—it's not in the W.A.S.P. culture. They don't even understand food! You know, many a night on white bread and diet Coke isn't exactly cuisine. So, if you say to a W.A.S.P. in the Republican party to treat the electorate as you would in the restaurant, what would their model be? IHOP? McDonalds, or Jack-in-the-Box? It wouldn't work! I don't think that would work, those models. A sane politician, though, would treat the electorate as if the electorate were customers in his restaurant.

Now, what does that mean? Let's say the Republicans are dying a miserable death because of the mishandling of everything, the worst public relations. They have an image problem you can't believe, and they mistreat their customer base. The customer base has told them for six years now, "We elected you to be conservative, not compassionate, so stop with the compassion already—particularly compassion for our enemy, compassion for illegal aliens from Mexico. Let's start with conservatism for our enemy and conservatism directed at illegal aliens." So, the base needs to be treated like customers in a restaurant who have been eating there for a number of years. What you do is you serve your base better than you do new customers, because if you lose your base then no matter how many new customers you get, you're going to go out of business.

47

ISLAMISTS ARE WINNING

The Dayton Peace Accords called for the removal of foreign combatants from Bosnia after the Balkans War, but hundreds of Mujahideen fighters stayed. Today they are successfully spreading their fundamentalist Islamist views.

By the way, they built a very large mosque in Sarajevo with Saudi money. What's strange here is that the Muslims of Bosnia were rather peaceful for a very long period of time and the Islamists are trying to turn them back to seventh century Muslim beliefs. There's a fight going on in Bosnia between modern Muslims and the throwbacks being funded by Saudi Arabia. The throwbacks are using violence against the moderate Muslims, who sometimes drive by the throwbacks and wave beer bottles at them as if to say, "You're not turning the clock back on us!" But Saudi Arabia is funding this Wahhabi sect of cancer—this cancerous Islamic sect of Wahhabism is being spread around the world right here in America! They fund CAIR. Make no mistake about what they are! Make no mistake about it.

Now, it is only a matter of time until the government finally recognizes that they're not going to win this battle through rhetoric alone. It is only a matter of time until you, the listener, realize that you're losing the war. The Muslims are winning the war! The Muslims, who are radical, are winning the war. By the way, the head of CAIR has been quoted as saying, "Sure, I'd like to see Sharia law in America." He's not going to force it down your throat. He says he's going to do it by slow increments. They're winning! They're winning!

Now during World War II, the Nazis worked on plans to build the American bomber. It was an airplane specifically devised to fly suicide missions into

Manhattan skyscrapers, says an article by Paul Belien. Albert Speer, the Nazi minister for armaments, recalled in his diary how Hitler seemed to get into a state of near delirium while describing his vision of New York in flames. The skyscrapers would turn into torches, he said, and crumble, all because Hitler hated Manhattan. According to him it was a central location for jewelry in the world. Less than 60 years later, Muslim immigrants living in Germany executed Hitler's plans. At the 2003 trial of the network of Mohamed Atta, the pilot who flew into the World Trade Center, Shahid Nickels, a German convert to Islam and a friend of Atta, said that the Islamists had targeted Manhattan because of the strong Jewish presence there and the financial and commercial control obtained by it.

The parallels between Nazism and Islamism are overwhelming—yet, the subject is a taboo. Last March Matthias Küntzel, German historian and author of *Jihad and Jew-Hatred: Islamism, Nazism, and the Roots of 9/11*, was to give a lecture at the University of Leeds in Britain. The university authorities cancelled the lecture after threats from Muslim students.

Ladies and gentlemen, I'm warning you that you're losing the war against radical Islam. They're putting a noose around your neck and they're tightening it! Now, most people don't want to talk about the radical Islamists. They'd rather put their heads in the sand. But, you know what? They're repeating history.

I was recently watching Ken Burns' great documentary on World War II. It made me think that America was very similar to today during the '30s: People didn't want to hear what was going on. They thought that they'd be spared the carnage of Europe. In the documentary he shows the little movie houses across America and the newsreels of the time. On a Saturday, the newsreels would show the carnage, for example, of the Spanish Civil War, the carnage of Germany invading Poland. It showed how the average Americans thought they would be spared involvement in World War II. They didn't want to be involved in it! They figured it wouldn't touch them, that we were isolationists at that time—that the country was actually pacifist and isolationist!

Then, they interviewed different people and started to talk about what finally turned them in the war. This I'll never forget: there's one guy from Sacramento who says he was a church-going guy, and he went into the military before World War II was declared, before the attack on Pearl Harbor. He said he signed up to go to the Philippines because he thought it was too far to be touched by the war. Well, lo and behold, the same day that Pearl Harbor was attacked by the Japanese imperialists, they also bombed and invaded a portion of the Philippines. They slowly started to strangle the Philippines. The U.S. troops moved further and further away from the point of contact because they were losing.

I am telling you, sure, we're all wanting to avoid the war with the radical Islamists. Sure, we want to turn our head away from this ugly, disgusting take-over of the world. We all want to turn away from it. We don't want to know about it, but we all know in our heart of hearts that it's going to touch us again. It touched us—remember?—on September 11, 2001. Remember that? They already struck us! Radical Islam is touching every military family in the country.

It's only a matter of time until the draft is reinstituted in America. It's going to have to be done, and the day the draft is instituted, there will be draft riots in the country, stimulated by the ACLU and other fellow traveler anti-Americans— we know that. We'll overcome them; they'll be jailed. There will be a draft in this country, and when that day comes, and Main Street is drawn into the war, I can guarantee you that the Islamists amongst us are either going to leave the country or be arrested by the FBI. It's only a matter of time and then you'll see that I was ahead of my time again.

48

ELECTION RESULTS, YEAR 2000
AND LEXUS LIBERALS

S tates that said, "Yes" to Bush: 38. States that said, "Yes" to Gore: 12.
Are some states more equal than other states? South Florida, for example,
the land of the New York Communistic front, with the millionaires grifting off
the welfare state; pretending to each other the moral indignation of the down-
trodden; acting with heads held high and jaws thrust out, as though they are personally victims of the Triangle Shirtwaist Fire.

Lexus liberals with Volkswagens on their brains; Condo commies; lunch room
Lenins; stand-up Stalins; miserable Maos; pathetic Pol-Pot Marxists. Stealing ballots,
grifting SSI, faking disabilities, voting for Al Gore. All in a day's work.

South Florida: the land of sunshine, schmoozing, and now, stupidity. The
whole world now knows New York Communist Democrats are too stupid to vote
straight but smart enough to twist the truth when their benefits are threatened.

South Florida: the land of suntanned Trotsky's in delis, bypassed Bolsheviks in
Buicks, air-conditioned Che's in condos, loud, lewd, losers in limbo—all stuck
between their investments and their liberalism. Lost to their religion; fervent in
their unbelief. "Save the DNC, their new religion." Corn beef commies; buffet
Bolsheviks; jogging jokesters—stuck in Camelot fantasies. Kennedy, their last
idol; Hillary, their personal Evita; Bill, their shameless shaygitz; Tipper, their tipsy
donut; Al, their Shabbos goy.

South Florida: the land of sun and S.O.Bs.

49

DEBUNKING MAN-INDUCED 'GLOBAL WARMING'

TOM: I'm calling to support the debunking global warming piece that you have on your homepage. I've worked with hundreds of climate scientists for the last 10 years in many countries. Frankly, there is no consensus about the causes of climate change. A lot of the stuff that we hear—and that the press tells us, unfortunately—is that there's this consensus and so many of the scientists are actually very reluctant to speak out. But what you're doing, and what others are doing, is hopefully creating a climate where more scientists can actually say what they're really finding.

SAVAGE: Yes, there is a box on michaelsavage.com called "Debunking Global Warming" and the headline says, "Less than half of published scientists endorse global warming theory." That doesn't stop charlatans like Al Gore from saying, "All scientists, virtually all scientists, agree." It doesn't stop politicians like Jerry Brown, the attorney general of the state of California, going on NPR two weeks ago and infuriating me by saying, "All scientists agree that global warming is real and is caused by man, and we now have to constrain industry in the hands of government." They don't permit anyone on NPR to get up there and say, "Now, wait a minute: less than half of published scientists endorse global warming theory."

It's amazing the big lie, but then, as Joseph Goebbels said, "When you tell a big lie often enough, it becomes the truth." Right now the globalists are telling the big lie through half-truths, which they sell as the whole truth.

TOM: And I'm saying to the media that frequently brings this up, I'm saying, "Prove it. Show us that there is a consensus in the climate science community"—

and they can't do it because there is no worldwide poll and the Gore crowd only represents a very small fraction of the world's scientists!

SAVAGE: A multi-national team of scientists worked for years. They bored 1.2 miles into the Greenland ice shelf. They removed the remnants, the DNA, of plants and animals that lived eons ago—and guess what they discovered? The earth was warmer eons ago than it is today! How can they then say that it's man who is causing this uptick in global warming? There may be an uptick in global warming, but it's not man who is doing it!

That is not to argue that I like pollution—I hate pollution! I'm a boater. I'm a hiker. I'm an outdoorsman. I despise people who poison the air and water, but I also despise liars who try to constrain industry around the Western world under the guise of global warming—and all in order to induce a soft Marxism: global control and global taxation.

50

STAPLE CUT ON PAPER:
Doctor Friend's Theory on Bloodletting

I t begins with a staple cut. I had to go to the laboratory this morning for a medical test, a blood test that I've been putting off for at least four weeks. Every day I've stared at the form: I wouldn't go. Every day I said, "I gotta go tomorrow and make sure when I get up I don't eat anything, don't take anything." So, I put it off every day, but I made up my mind today was going to be the day. I went down the driveway in the morning in my bathrobe to get the paper. I picked it up and took it out of its blue wrapper, and I tried to rip a notice attached to the paper, which said, "Merry Christmas. My name is Jose. Could you please leave me a gift in this envelope?" And I cut my finger on a staple, so my finger bled. What a bad start to the day.

You know, you give the newspaper guy some money. The guy comes in the middle of the night—why not? You throw him a $20 bill, a $50 bill—who knows what we give him. I don't know. I never stiff anybody. I know what it's like to be almost a slave in this country.

I went to the lab, got the butterfly, the six vials of blood. I never felt better! I'll tell you, maybe there's something to bloodletting that we have to look into. I have an 80-year-old doctor friend who is very healthy. He is an orthomolecular physician who bleeds himself on a regular basis. He swears it's a very healthy thing to do. So, I said, "What's your theory about bleeding yourself? Why is it a healthy thing to do?"

"Well for one, it removes the iron from a man's blood to a certain extent. As you well know, iron can be somewhat toxic with regard to coronary heart disease."

I said, "Well, what's the natural evidence that you have?"

"Well, it's very simple, Michael. Throughout history, in primitive times, mankind had to hunt. Mankind had to fight, and often he bled. He bled small amounts of blood on a fairly regular basis, whether he was hunting in the brush and cutting himself on the brush, or in a fight with an animal, or in a fight with another human being. And he bled, and it was good for him."

Today, in these frightened times, if a drop of blood comes out of our bodies, we get paranoid and go to the doctor and get "treated"—or, we spray ourselves. It's an interesting thought, related to the newspaper, the driveway, and the staple. I thought I would share it with you.

51

HORMONES AND STEROIDS IN FOODS; ABORTION AND CANCER

SAVAGE: Florida, Jeff. You're on "The Savage Nation." What's on your mind, sir?

JEFF: Well, Michael, God bless you for your work. I'm a retired holistic physician out here in northeast Florida. I had a radio show downstream of you for a couple of years, but I had to go low-profile because, I want to tell you—I'm voting for you to go to the Asian buffet, the Asian restaurant in Las Vegas. I'll tell you why. You talk about the homosexualization of America and you talk about—. I'm a neurologist and a psychiatrist, retired. Why are these people looking at porn? Why are they passing porn? Why are men becoming effeminate in this country?

SAVAGE: Because they're not eating enough Italian food.

JEFF: Well, unfortunately, they need heavy foods, but they need it to be without all the steroids, without all the pesticides, without all the toxic chemicals.

SAVAGE: I hear what you're saying. You're saying that foods that are full of hormones are feminizing men. Isn't that what you're arguing?

JEFF: Right. Research at the University of Florida already showed that some of our poor alligators are being born without you-know-whats because there's so much estrogen-like pesticides in our food supply.

SAVAGE: Oh my! Even alligators are being born like liberals?

JEFF: Exactly. You and I have so much in common. I've been reading through most of your books. I started out working in the pharmacy, the whole nine yards.

SAVAGE: Are you a retired psychiatrist?

JEFF: Retired neurology and psychiatry. But what I really spent my time doing—

SAVAGE: This is interesting. Where did you go to medical school?

JEFF: Pennsylvania State University College of Medicine, Hershey, Pennsylvania.

SAVAGE: That is a great school. You were a smart kid, right? You knew what you were doing from the beginning.

JEFF: I was much smarter than that. I went to the Benjamin Franklin School for Undergraduate, the University of Pennsylvania. Know what I learned? I learned I needed to listen with respect to everyone—never become an egomaniac; keep an open mind.

While you were traveling around the world collecting plants, I was learning everything I could about Chinese medicine and chiropractic and organic farming, and hanging out with those people. I'm telling you that after World War II, when these German chemical companies took over in combination with all these oil companies—took over our economy—I want you to know, I'm a conservative Republican now, but when they took over and started feeding our population all these steroids in the meat and all these estrogens and pesticides—

The only reason I'm calling tonight is that you're one of the last voices on the radio left from an era when people weren't being poisoned by all these foods.

SAVAGE: That's really funny. That's an amazing story. What you're saying is that in the age that I grew up in, in the formative years that my brain was being laid down, the foods were not laden with the chemicals. Is that what you're saying?

JEFF: Exactly. An Italian man had to have the courage to say, "Wheat is so full of pesticides now." He had to tell his Italian family to stop eating the pasta and switch over to rice. He wrote a book called, *Eat Right for Your Type.* It has to do with your blood type, your immune system—

SAVAGE: Well, you see, here's where you and I digress a little, Jeff. I come from the holistic medical background in the Ph.D. side from University of California at Berkeley. The problem is, when you get so rarified in your dietary needs, I think that's another form of extremism, the rarification.

For example, a lot of people will only give their dogs bottled water. I think that's ludicrous! At a certain point, you've got to drink a little tap water and give your dog a little tap water. You're not going to die from it in every community in America! Moreover, your body has to get used to it.

Wasn't I talking yesterday about the strength of Ukrainian athletes, particularly the boxers? These guys grew up on virtually poisonous food in the Ukraine, and they're strong as iron. So, I'm not so sure that rarified diets necessarily are the only way to go, Jeff.

JEFF: You're talking to a Ukrainian Jew with a Ukrainian wife fresh over from Ukraine five years ago.

SAVAGE: What, she hasn't killed you yet?

JEFF: She tried to kill me two years ago, but we're both Jewish Christians so we decided to give it another shot. Now, we've got a beautiful baby.

SAVAGE: So, you're 55 and she's 25?

JEFF: I'm 51 and she's 30.

SAVAGE: Well, I wasn't too far off. I knew it! You're still breathing?

JEFF: I'm still breathing—I've got three kids!

SAVAGE: Well, you must be eating something right, Jeff.

JEFF: I know your family goes back to the Ukraine. That's why you're so smart.

SAVAGE: Well, no, wait. Is Minsk in the Ukraine?

JEFF: It's all the same. It's all volcanic rock, good food, no pesticides.

SAVAGE: Let me tell you something: I don't think the Ukrainians—but, you know, the food my ancestors ate was pretty poor. They lived on grains. They had very little meat. They were very poor for centuries. Maybe that's what made them smart and strong. You know, one of the food staples of that area for a long period of time was called "buckwheat." Do you know that or not?

JEFF: Yes, yes.

SAVAGE: I love buckwheat. You can't find it! Can you find buckwheat today? You know, you talk about Asian food—one of my favorite Japanese soups is a soup made with buckwheat noodles. For the $24 question, what's the name of that soup?

JEFF: Miso.

SAVAGE: No, no, no! Not miso soup. You're the expert, you see. There's a noodle made of buckwheat that is served in a certain Japanese soup. It's very hard to find: it's soba. Soba is very hard to find in America properly cooked. The buckwheat noodle is worth getting. What a great caller.

In other news, abortion is fueling the cancer epidemic. Having an abortion raises a woman's risk of breast cancer by at least 30 percent, according to a major study by British researchers—and it's published in a major journal, that an abortion in a young woman who's never had a child has a carcinogenic effect. You don't want to hear this, many of you Leftists, but it's a reality. The people who are fighting it are those in the American Cancer Society and those in the abortion rackets. For years, medical professionals have seen a linkage between abortions and cancer in women.

MENTAL ILLNESS

SAVAGE: Debbie, San Francisco. Go ahead.

DEBBIE: Yes, sir. Dr. Savage, I do suffer from psychological and psychiatric illness, and I denied it for many, many years, having heard stories of my grandmother in New York, who stripped naked at a parade after just being released from a psychiatric hospital. She was a little too happy and was returned by black wagon to suffer another round of electroshock therapy.

So, growing up, when I found myself suffering from similar "symptomologies," I refused to go get help.

SAVAGE: So, what is your main point? Of course there's mental illness—there've always been marginally crazy people and overtly crazy people. We know that, so what is it that we're disagreeing on?

DEBBIE: I think it's not subjective, sir. I think that there is a scientific way of producing diagnoses by way of examining common symptoms and behavior.

SAVAGE: Well, it's not that precise. That's the point, and that's where the rub lies. The doctors would have you believe that it's easy to definitively diagnose mental illness: I disagree entirely. It's not that easy.

Now, I've seen brain-scan studies—don't get me wrong. I've seen different colorations in schizophrenics and others, but we have no fundamental argument here. In other words, I know there are people who are unstable; I know there are people who are totally crazy; and I know people who are rock-steady and never suffer any such orientation.

So, where the argument arises is, can we control some of these proclivities through means other than medication? That is the only argument I think we're having.

DEBBIE: Well, I definitely think it can be controlled through medication. The disappointment though—

SAVAGE: You didn't hear me. You see? You went right over what I said! I said, "Can some of these symptoms or conditions be controlled with means other than medication?"

DEBBIE: I think it depends on, to what extent an individual is suffering. In my case, the answer is "No." I spent many, many years seeking out—I went to Marin County, I saw the best nutritional therapists, and I wish I could say their names on the air.

SAVAGE: Did you try mega-doses? I'm going to pick one thing out of there. Did you try massive doses of Niacin?

DEBBIE: Sir, I tried Niacin until my skin was so red that I looked like—

SAVAGE: I'm only asking because I want to know how far you went along with nutritional therapies. Of course, they're not going to work in all cases—but you did try Dr. Hoffer's mega doses of Niacin?

DEBBIE: I had more Niacin in my blood. I went to Oregon; I went to LA. I had neurosurgery for a very bizarre—

SAVAGE: And they looked at your iron levels? They looked at your folic acid levels, correct?

DEBBIE: Everything. I had more blood panels drawn from me and—

SAVAGE: Alright, so you went that route; that route didn't help you, and now you're on major anti-psychotic drugs. And you feel better, correct?

DEBBIE: I absolutely feel better.

SAVAGE: Well, no one's arguing with that, but I'm saying don't put children on Ritalin the minute they show signs of being a boy.

DEBBIE: I absolutely agree with that.

SAVAGE: Alright, so there's no argument. You'll get me crazy if I keep talking to you another three minutes—three more minutes and I'll need to reach for a pill!

I once went and visited a holy man, a religious teacher. He was a former boxer who then went into religion, but he still maintained the mentality of the "man of the street." He knew reality, in other words. I was suffering at the time through various stresses that were going on in my life, mainly societal social engineering that made me feel like a failure because I was not granted what I had earned. They wanted to employ people with less qualifications instead: people of other races and other sexual orientations. (Total morons, by the way, given jobs—which is why the university has fundamentally collapsed in America, in many departments; but certainly not in the scenes where social engineering is minimal.)

I didn't know what was wrong. I sacrificed to earn my Ph.D. My master's thesis was published in a Harvard University journal. My doctoral thesis was published as a book. Yet, universities preferred to hire 20-watt people from countries of origin other than the United States of America, to make them feel good and to make them look good on the brochures.

So I went to see this holy man. He asked me, "What exactly is your problem?"

I explained it to him, and he said, "You know, we have a saying that if you take a stick and put it into dog shit, no matter which way you turn the stick, it's still dog shit." Then he said, "Now if you don't mind, I'll have to excuse myself right now."

I got very mad at him—I was fuming because I wanted some mystical experience in this holy man's office. He told me that if you take a stick and you put it in you-know-what, no matter how you move the stick around, it's still you-know-what! What he was telling me was, "Stop moving the stick around in your own psychic waste"—and he was right.

So, there are many ways to cure problems. Not all require "medication." Sometimes common sense works. That's what I'm trying to tell you, that there's an epidemic of a "loss of common sense." We have a nation of weaklings! "Medication, medication, I'm on my medication. I want my crutch. I want my drugs. I'm on my medication. I want Uncle Sam to pay for my medication. I'm sickly. I want my drug."

Well, maybe you need your drug, and maybe you don't. Maybe you're just a weak individual who refuses to take control of your own life. You know, maybe you're diabetic, yet you're still eating donuts? I wouldn't give you medication: I'd make you pay for your medication if you refused to modify your diet! If you're not willing to help yourself, why should I help you? That's one reason our taxes are out of control in this country, but, more than that, psychiatry is often used as mind-control, societal-control.

We're moving very, very close to the ex-Soviet Union, where psychiatrists were used to diagnose citizens as "anti-social" or "anti-political." They were then taken away by the secret police, medicated into submission, and thrown into re-education camps. If you think we're not moving in that direction, my friend, you are mistaken.

Some well-meaning psychiatrists are not far from recommending that political dissonance be medicated, that anyone who suffers certain political orientations or beliefs can only be treated with major pharmaceuticals. And I can guarantee you as I sit here that it's going to come from the homosexual radical community, that "Christians who believe in the Word of God are psychiatrically impaired, by definition, and they should be medicated and they should be re-educated: that is the only way to cure them of their God-madness." I can guarantee you it's being whispered in psychiatric halls!

I see what's coming in this country unless you stand up to this juggernaut of the medical legal profession—or, I should say, the medical/pharmaceutical/legal profession because they're all intimately involved. Now, that's not to throw away all of medicine. That would be foolish, and I've never said that. That would be a ridiculous thing to say. I'm talking about integrative medicine, where all of these modalities work together. I refuse to be led around by the nose into believing that there are no ways to affect the mind and body other than through pharmaceuticals. The drug establishment is out of control!

Take a look at the Viagra ads. I turned on Fox, CNN, MSNBC. I flipped around the 15-minutes-after-the-hour all day, and all I saw was a white-haired man dancing a woman around on the floor with a big smile as they left to go to the hotel room and said, "Viagra, Viagra, Viagra." Every channel at 15-after-the-hour: "every man over the age of 40 needs Viagra," according to the advertisements. Could it be that the man is impotent—excuse me, "erectile dysfunctional"—because he really doesn't want to have sex, because he's not in heat? We are the only animal on earth that is diluted by our societal images and pressures into thinking that we should be ready for sex 24/7.

"Wow, I'm rarin' to go 365 days a year. I can spring up like a 15 year old. I'm a potent man." There's no animal on earth that is potent 365 days a year. We're the only animals who've been fooled into thinking that we should be! So now we medicate the fact that we're not desirous of sex. Perhaps we're out of sync with desire, or we shouldn't be having sex at all right now. Why must a man have sex 365 days a year? Where have you read of an animal that has sex 365 days a year? It's unheard of! So, in a sense, we are a totally insane society, being led around by advertisements.

53

SEPARATE BEDROOMS

I read a story once about the number of married couples in the U.S. that choose to sleep in separate bedrooms. A survey showed that this trend is increasingly popular because of marital tension and disturbances in sleep as a result of sharing a bedroom. They're not calling it a separate bedroom because the people are embarrassed to admit it. They call it a "flex suite" instead, to avoid any embarrassment.

Let me tell you a little secret about that: it's only poor couples who sleep in the same bed for their whole lives, generally. Not everybody, don't get me wrong. But generally it's a mark of poverty to have to share a bed with someone your whole life.

The fact of the matter is, if you study the history of this—let's start with royalty. They never shared the same bedroom, never mind the same bed! We're not talking about in the beginning phases, when they were in the 90 days of marital heat—that's an understood fact. The 90-day period is over after 90, 91 days according to every study that's ever been done. Ninety days of insanity, then by 91 days it's already over. It goes on to a certain extent, but after 90 days you have to live with this person.

So, first it starts out as twin beds in the same room, very close to each other, with a little nightstand. Then it's not so much twin beds: you get the bigger beds in the same room. Then if you have a little money. . . . That's how it works; that's the fact of the matter. There's no shame in it! You can still get together when you want, but you have two different lives, two different minds. Why do you have to share every second in the bedroom? What, that's some sacred place to be together? The way people are today, individually, they don't want to be in the same room—and, by the way, this is not limited to America. I'll give you an example, an anthropological experience about men and women.

In Fiji—let's go back to the years I was living in Fiji, in the village. This is a delicate subject. The men had a men's house and the women had a women's house. When a woman went through her monthly cycles, she went into the women's house with the other women. The men didn't want to be around them during that time! Now, what does that make the men in Fiji? Does it make them sexist? Does it make them whatever "—ist" you want to call it? They knew, from their culture, that they didn't want to be around the women at that time, for whatever the reasons were. And I got news for you: the women would rather be with their friends at that time, too! So, the guys went over with their friends in their separate house, they all hung out, slept in the same big straw hut—and the women slept together! That's how they did it in Fiji. I'm giving you one example.

So, this whole idea of how to raise a child—or how to live with a woman or, for a woman, how to live with a man—there's no set rules in this area. A lot of what we see going on today is devolution, not evolution. The people don't even actually understand how to live with each other or how to raise children. And what they always do is to try the liberal methodology: people think that by going with liberal social mores it's going to work, and it often doesn't.

What you have to do is go back to the traditional methods of raising children and the traditional methods of living in the same household—man and woman, woman and man.

54

MOVIE THEATRES

D.J.: I'm only 26 years old. I can't relax in a restaurant, but what about a movie theatre? Those are the worst for me. I just cringe because right when I sit down, I see a family with five or six kids that just want to talk throughout the whole thing.

SAVAGE: Yeah, they think it's their personal video experience in their living room. In my day, we had ushers that went around with flashlights, and they put it in your eyes if you talked. It didn't always work, you know—we mocked the ushers and threw candy at them. We weren't all dolls, believe me, but we knew not to talk because the other kids would have wanted to fight us if we talked. We had self-control because the audience would have controlled us otherwise.

D.J.: I look around and it's like I'm the only one that cares. The audience doesn't seem to care! It's like I'm weird because I'm upset that parents want to—

SAVAGE: I seldom go to a movie. I try to go very late at night or—I went to two movies in the whole year. That's why I watch movies at home. What do you expect in a movie theatre? The lowest common denominator is in a movie theatre, not the highest. They're not generally working people. Ever see them lining up at 12:30, the Social Security crowd? You don't want to be in there after a Medicare meal, I'll tell you that, because they cut back on the air conditioning. You could die in those theatres!

I had it happen in the elevator last week in the building I'm in. You don't want to go in those elevators! Some conglomerate from Boston owns them. I'm in San Francisco and, to save on electricity, they told the management not to put the fan on in the elevator. You could just die! If you get in, the wrong time of day, after the seniors have taken Metamucil, you take your life in your hands in the elevator! What are you going to do? I don't mean when they're in there with you.

I'm talking about after they get out and you get in, and the elevator starts to climb. What are you going to do at that point? It's like San Quentin, like the gas chamber! I mean, there's nothing you can do—you're finished at that point! You're stuck for a certain number of floors. You come out with your eyes smarting and gagging—but that's people today. They don't care. What do they care if the next guy's going to come in and gag? They actually do it on purpose.

55

THE TWO FACES OF ENGLAND

Many of the Brits admit that their country is depraved and sick, and we could say the same of the U.S., really. On the other hand, guidebooks describe a quaint society, where tea and crumpets are served each day at the same time and people wear tweeds in the country and trains generally run on time.

For me, the only problem with the English is they can't speak the language properly. That's the one problem with them. They never kept up with the times. They kept a brittle, older language that doesn't really resemble the English that I know. It doesn't work for them anymore, and that's why they're shriveling as a nation!

People don't like that. That British accent was hot in the '60s. Everyone hired a chick that had a British accent. All the Jewish guys in the garment center really got hot for that. You know what I mean? "Yeah, Mr. Katz is not here." They always hired them in the garment center—that's who they hired. But that's over with. Now they want an African or a Mexican.

If you've got someone who speaks a kind of immigrant English it's more appealing in a certain way, very in your face. No one wants that proper English accent. That's over. In the '60s, yes, right through the late '50s and early '60s: Twiggy, the Beatles, the Aston Martin—the whole thing was very cool. But then the English thing died, with the breakdown of the nation; with immigration; because of the asylum and the liberalism; from floods of immigrants with the welfare system. England is not England anymore. But what is?

56

POLITICAL MUSEUMS AND DOWNFALL OF WESTERN CULTURE

Question is this: do you still go to museums or have museums become "museums" in the U.S.A.? I went to a museum in San Francisco the other day. I haven't been there for five or six years. I used to live in museums. Because I grew up in my dad's antique store looking at art, I spent a lot of time in museums—I always have. I stopped going years ago, though, when the AIDS racketeers started dominating San Francisco's collections and turned everything in museums into a sort of "plea" for a special sub-population of the American people. I couldn't take it anymore, so I stopped going.

Too many exhibits were propaganda, not art. They put a basket from Guatemala next to a Rembrandt and they tell you they're culturally equal! You hear? Nevertheless, the European collections are still there—and they still stand out, and they are still worth going to see.

So, let me begin at the end: I left the museum after two hours and came out feeling enlightened. I use the word "enlightened" in the way it truly was written and meant to be understood: I felt lighter inside. My spirit was lifted from association with great art. I stood nose to nose with Hopper and Church and other great artists—you know, the sight an inch from the oil paint is an astonishing thing to behold. You can literally feel the movements of the brush. It does something to your mind that you can't compare with anything else—certainly not television or a movie.

So, I saw some of my favorite old paintings. They were amazingly fabulous. I just love the intelligent, young families with young children: sadly, they're mainly Europeans, I must tell you. There are very few American families; it's mainly French families that still take their young children to the museums, as I did my children.

Now I'm going to mention a "yenta." A yenta is a term in American slang denoting a "busybody." There was an exhibit in the museum that was just breathtakingly, frighteningly hard to believe it was in a museum, about this San Franciscan-native yenta with good taste in fashion. When I saw this I thought, *Now this can't be. They can't be doing this.* But, yes, they were doing it. Here's a woman I never heard of and her dresses were in showcases in the museum! But wait, it gets worse: there was a whole glass case devoted to this woman's shoes. Her shoes! So, I stood there laughing out loud. People thought I was crazy! I said, "My God, it's every yenta's dream. There they are, the yenta's shoes, under glass in a museum after she's dead."

So, a guard came over to me and whispered, "You're 100 percent right. Don't tell anyone I said so." He couldn't believe it, either! I said, "In all the years you've been in a museum, have you ever seen a woman's shoes put on display in a showcase?" He said, "Never." So I said, "This exhibit is the ultimate 'nothing.'" It's the ultimate nothing. You have to ask yourself, "Who is in charge of our museums, that they would put a woman's dresses in the showcase—and her shoes?"

This woman was living on her father's money and her husband's money—probably did nothing in her life except wear clothing. I'm editorializing, mind you: this is my opinion. This was in a major museum in the U.S.A. in the year 2007! This is what it's come down to, with the assault upon our institutions in this country by the illegitimate Left. This is the kind of garbage they're showing! They put this exhibit in an American museum, next to paintings by Hopper, paintings by Church, paintings by the most genius artists of our historical past. They put a yenta's clothing in a showcase.

I could not believe that this is what has become considered worthy of showing in our museums. How did this happen to American culture? Would you like to give me the answer or would you like Mike to give *you* the answer? Now remember, I grew up in museums. I spent many, many, many a happy rainy day playing hooky at the Metropolitan Museum in New York—thousands of hours in the Metropolitan, wandering, before it became a zoo. Wandering alone on rainy Tuesdays, or Wednesdays, or Thursdays, in soiled raincoats; wandering the endless halls before it filled up with the Euro- hordes and forced school children; wandering through these halls of the museums.

It does not make me an art expert by any means, but then, there are no art experts. The fact of the matter is, there are people who are expert in certain areas of art and they could probably tell you something about a painting that you don't already know, but, ultimately, you're the best judge of whether a piece of art is really a piece of art. You are the only judge of whether a piece of art is a piece of art! It's the average man who is the judge. It's not the effete, academic, who will determine whether a piece of art is a piece of art anymore than an academic can tell you whether a baseball player is really a great baseball player. It's the fan in the stadium that will tell you whether he's a great baseball player, not the guy writing for the newspaper!

I need a day in the museum, I thought before going. The positive side of this outing was seeing the great paintings by Hopper, the great paintings by Church, the great paintings by so many other artists that I grew up salivating over. After seeing these, I must tell you, I wandered into the Oceania Collection, which is the Pacific Islands collection. I spent many years during my time in the South Pacific collecting mud masks and shields, and I am talking about collecting them in the late '60s and early '70s, when they were really exquisite. They were museum pieces. I have them somewhere—I don't even know where I put them—in storage.

When you walk around the Oceania collection—I'm talking about the Pacific Islands: Polynesia, Melanesia, Micronesia, the islands of the deep South Pacific and the western Pacific. When I walk around and look at these death masks in the showcases—where there are human skulls in a showcase called "ancestral masks," where they take the head, the skull of an ancestor, put feathers and mud around it, and put it in their house as a totem—a number of thoughts and feelings come to my mind. A) They're spooky and eerie, and the person is in there and I can feel the person's spirit in the showcase, and B) they don't belong in the showcase. They should be returned to New Guinea where they came from.

If the Greeks or Romans or Italians can demand their art back from the crooks at the Getty Museum then certainly the poor people of New Guinea can demand to get back the masks that contain actual skulls from people who lived. Know what I'm saying? But let me get to the next point—

You stand there and look at some of these Oceanic art works. First, you can dismiss them as primitive and not really great if you don't really understand what they are, but if you do understand what they are, you actually see the greatness in some of these pieces of mud and feathers and bone and shell. Now, that's an area that I really could talk about for ages because I spent a lot of time looking at those things.

The power of "primitive" art is great—and I'm not talking about the garbage that they carve in the Philippines now for the tourists or the junk that they're selling in the streets of Tahiti. That's all junk. I'm talking about the stuff that was collected, let's say, up to 1920, or even 1940. Pre-World War II art out of the Oceania area is astonishing in terms of its power as transmitted by the artists.

57

DO PEOPLE GO TO PLAYS AND SYMPHONIES ANYMORE?

D o you go to plays anymore? Why would you go to a play when you can watch television? Is that "culture" just because it's in a theatre with bad seats and you actually hear people coughing? That makes it "theatre," higher art than television? Let's talk about that for a minute since we're talking about "what's art and what's not art," "what's poetry and what's not poetry," in an age of a collapsed civilization where everybody can call themselves an artist or a poet.

What is the difference if you sit home and watch a movie—and it's a very well-done movie, let's say, or you go to a "theatre" to watch *Don Giovanni* at the Metropolitan Opera? How many times can audiences watch *Don Giovanni* at an opera house, with the same plot over and over again? Why are they going to see *Don Giovanni?* I'd rather watch *Serpico* than watch *Don Giovanni.* I can pause it, I can get up and go to the bathroom, I don't have to smell anyone's perfume. I don't have to sit there stiff, making believe I'm enjoying every word. Then they put in the super titles—that's in case you don't know a word of Italian. Even Italians don't understand many phrases in *Don Giovanni!* It's from another age.

I gave up on opera 10 years ago. You'd go in, the same stiff, boring audience; the same six or ten plays, either in Italian or German, over and over again; the same boring plots. How can you sit through that?

I'm not into high culture: I don't like any of it. I don't like the symphony at all—I can't stand it! I do not like symphony. Am I allowed to admit that to you? I cannot stand symphonic productions. I find them overwrought; I find them painful to sit through. It all collapsed for me when I found out what was going on in the world of music. You want to hear that now?

145

It happened here in San Francisco about 12 to 15 years ago: the San Francisco symphony, which was once at least a B-symphony, is now less than an F-symphony. When it was still a B-symphony it decided that it didn't have enough people of color and enough women playing. Tryouts were previously conducted behind a black curtain. Let's say a violinist was trying out for the symphony: she would play for three judges who sat behind a black curtain. They didn't know who was playing. They listened to the violinists, to the sound of the music: "Alright, number one, number two, number three, number four." The "number three" violinist is the best, so they pull back the curtain. They didn't care who got it. So, OK: another white male. Sorry, he was the best.

Well, the white males were winning too many of these positions in the symphony, so they took the curtain away. "We've got to make the symphony look like America," they said. Know what it sounds like today? The seventh grade! A warm-up job! That was the end of that kind of music for me.

Now, I'm not knocking music; I didn't say that. I'm saying the opera that I used to go to, the opera performances that I have seen in San Francisco or even in New York, left me cold. I got nothing out of them. Where do you go to get great opera?

A caller once said, "Well, I was privileged to hear the Three Tenors down in Miami and—"

SAVAGE: Yeah, but that's kind of schmaltzy. It's like opera for the masses. Everyone has his own taste. I went to an opera I'll never forget: it was many years ago in Italy, at the Baths of Caracalla on a hot, summer night. I'll never forget as long as I live when they brought out the white horses with the wagon on the stage. Now, that was dramatic! When I saw opera in Italy—I'm talking 30 years ago in the Baths of Caracalla in an outdoor amphitheatre—that knocked me over! OK? Could have been the wine, I don't really know. Could have been my companion—I was a different person then. Now I'm a reformed personality, but today, what opera house has anything? Different strokes for different folks: I'll be liberal about it.

58

NEW YORK TIMES AD:
Sex Doesn't Sell

The Style section of a newspaper caught my eye one day because it showed women in very '50s-like outfits. It said something like, "Sex no longer selling." Modest clothing—high-neck dresses and knee-length skirts, for example—are back in style, instead. I thought it was interesting because I've been saying, "We're saturated with the thongs"—you know, since Clinton, the degenerate, with the thong thing. I never liked thongs. It's unsanitary just looking at them! I gag looking at a thong. Who would want something stuck in your behind like that? I never understood who would wear a thing like that. As a man, I would never wear something that was stuck—

The ad said some of the top designers are saying, essentially, that the styles of the '50s are the new sexy. Yes, that's exactly true. They're actually sexier. The ad goes on to say that the trend will not fade quickly because the average American no longer desires the look of low-cut jeans and tight blouses and visible thongs, blah, blah, blah.

So, women, what do you think? Do you want crinolines? Do you want blouses with bows? Are you sick of the thong? The belly button ring?

I think it's easier on the women, to be frank with you, to not have to dress like the slut from the *E!* channel. Is it easier on you to dress in crinolines and blouses and bows? I don't know. It looks like my deceased aunt. I just hope they don't bring back the fur with those foxes and the faces. Those things scared me as a kid. Now we're going way back; that's another story. Forget the '50s. We're talking about my grandmother, may she rest in peace.

She had a fur piece with a fox on it. She'd come in from the cold. A mixture of the cold fur and her perfume gave me a migraine. I'm sure my migraines started with her perfume. God rest her soul—I don't mean any disrespect. I would be frightened because I was a little kid. Up to the fox's head it looked like a real fox. She'd come in and then the women of the family would go talk in the kitchen. I don't know, I guess they'd eat coffee cake, give themselves diabetes and heart attacks. God only knows the poison they put in their bodies! I would hang out in the living room and get hung up on that fox's face, with the little teeth. I remember to this day rubbing my little five-year-old fingers along the teeth of the fox. I don't want to go back to those horrendous days.

59

PLASTIC BAGS BANNED IN SAN FRANCISCO, BUT NOT CONDOMS

Politicians are so full of crap. Here in San Francisco, for example, they banned plastic bags in supermarkets. They said it's bad for the environment because the plastic bags don't deteriorate or disintegrate; they sit in the landfill for thousands of years. They're very concerned about the *environment* in San Francisco, so now you have to bring a paper bag when you go into a supermarket. If you're walking out in the rain, it doesn't matter to the socialists who run the city.

Paper bags, of course, disintegrate in the rain and your groceries get wet. The plastic was much better and much more convenient, but let's take it on the face of it. So, plastic isn't biodegradable. Then how come they distribute *condoms* in San Francisco like M&Ms? Aren't those made of plastic? You're telling me that condoms don't sit in landfills for 20,000 years? You see the hypocrisy and stupidity?

We are also told that the salmon population is dying out; that the salmon are not breathing. We don't read that the people are not breathing—only that the salmon are not breathing. So, now they're going to spend hundreds of millions of dollars because it could mean severe fishing restrictions otherwise. Then they try to analyze why the spawning, the number of salmon that are spawning, has decreased. Nobody will say that perhaps the toxic garbage that is dumped offshore is poisoning the oceans; nobody will say that the hospital waste and the other untreated sewage that goes out into the ocean is so toxic that it's killing the fisheries off the coast of California. Oh, no! Instead, they'll tell you to cut out plastic bags in the supermarket.

60

WHAT IF JOHN MCCAIN'S MIDDLE NAME WAS 'JESUS'?

So, we spent an hour talking about Barak Hussein Obama, and I asked a question: "Why is his middle name an irrelevant question? What is Hussein? Where'd he get the name? Why is it not right to ask the question?" And I posed the question: "What if John McCain's middle name was 'Jesus'? What if it was John *Jesus* McCain? Don't you suppose the liberals would be saying, "Well, what does that mean? Do you want to convert us all? Are you a fanatic Christian, Mr. McCain?" If it was John *Jesus* McCain they'd be asking that question, but with Barak *Hussein* Obama: "How dare you ask that question!"

By the way, Mr. Romney's Mormonism became an issue to the radicals—but not Barry Hussein's Islamic background (His father was a Muslim; his African half-brother is a Muslim).

You know, Obama looks like Alfred E. Newman with those big ears. He's not a very good-looking guy. I told you a thousand times: it's not about the fact that he's multi-racial to me. I would vote for a black man in a second if he were a conservative. You have to take me at my word! I'd vote for a black woman if she could save America! I don't care what the person's race is. I don't happen to like this man's socialist policy papers and speeches; I don't happen to like the bag-men that he's been associated with in Chicago; I don't like the fact that he has a nasty wife who seems to have a distemper for America and thinks it's only good now that her husband's getting attention.

Now, I recognize that many think he walks on water and that he can cure diseases if you just go to one of his rallies—but I'm not one of them.

61

DAY OFF

Yesterday was a day that looked like I did nothing: I took the day off to catch my breath and then at night, as I went to sleep, I said, "You know, this was a remarkable day!" What did I do? Nothing. It started out on the beach. I needed to get some air. I happen to live in Northern California near San Francisco. There's a tunnel under the headlands of Marin County that you can drive through and be at the beach in 10 minutes. It's an old ammunition tunnel, by the way. I don't know how many of the people who ride bicycles through there know that, but the tunnel was built as an ammo tunnel for the military in World War II.

So, I went out on the beach. It was a gloomy, cold day. I walked and walked and walked and collected flat rocks. As I picked up these absolutely smooth, flat rocks, I remembered they were once hills. I thought to myself as I walked as a spirit through time, *Doesn't that take a little of the pressure off you to realize that these rocks were once mountains and that you're just merely a man walking through time?*

So, I got back to my real self, the naturalist self. After doing that, I went to an Indian lunch buffet. You say, "Well, what's remarkable about that?" Well, I'll tell you what's remarkable about that: normally I go to these and eat the vegetables—maybe also a little of the Tandori chicken—and try to avoid the lamb. You know, $8.95, all-you-can-eat. I'm not a fat guy, so I eat one plate and maybe go back for another small serving.

I got there at 1:45 p.m. and they close at 2. Scattered few tables talking; that was it. Everyone was through eating. I said, "Could you put more lamb in there?" I was in the lamb mood. I never eat it—I feel bad for the animal. I don't like the high-fat diet. I knocked off a plate; there was nothing but bones left. I'd been sick and I really needed the carotene and the fat and the B$_{12}$—I was craving it. There was grease on my hands and face. I took my food into the back room so that no one could watch me eat—I really wanted to enjoy myself. So, the Indian guy who owns it—I saw in the second pass when the bones were rising in the plate—I saw his eye was going up already, he saw a money loser. In the middle of the buffet, the phone rings. My hands are greasy. Now, this is a tough one: you have two greasy hands and a greasy mouth. The phone rings, and I knew it was a U.S. Congressman calling. I knew I had to take the call. I had given my number out to his assistant because he said he had to call me about something.

I took the call. "Hello, Congressman. How are you?"

"Michael," he said, "Do you remember a few months back you said you would help the combat vets when they came back from Iraq?"

I said, "Yes."

He said, "Well, there's some wonderful combat veterans running for office, and I agreed to help them."

It was Congressman Duncan Hunter. We had a great conversation—I'll tell you more about that at another time. I'm giving you a day now, a day in the life of Michael Savage. I went home, took a nap, then I went out to dinner that night. I was going to go; I wasn't gonna go; then I was. I couldn't make up my mind. Then I went. I had dinner with two remarkable men: one is a very close friend of mine, maybe my only friend. He is an inventor, a philanthropist, Maurice Kanbar. He drives me crazy; I drive him crazy—but we love each other because we love each other. That's all there is to it.

The other man is a new friend of mine: he's a producer, a film producer/director/writer by the name of Rupert Hitzig. He did one of my favorite movies of all time, *Wolfen*. Years ago he did *Electra Glide in Blue*. He did *Jaws 3-D*. Rupert loves my show; he says I'm one of the greatest storytellers he's ever heard—and he's heard them all. He's worked with Alan King, he's worked with really talented men in the entertainment business. He says, "Really, you're unbelievable. When you tell a story, no one can top you."

Except, he topped me. We're having pizza and a little soup and a salad, and he starts to tell me a story, when I said, "Are you making this up?" I can't tell you the whole story right now; I'm giving an overview. His mother and father had seven children, and then after the seven children the mother ran off with Rupert's violin teacher and married him.

I said, "What? That's impossible. That can't happen!"

Now, how we got there is because he said, "You're a great storyteller. I remember the story you were telling about Lido Beach, Long Beach: little house; the half-man, half-woman; the bronzes." He said, "I grew up there. My step-father was Italian. We lived in the Italian enclave out in Long Beach, where it was half Mafia."

I said, "Tell me the rest of this—are you making it up?" I looked it up on Google: it turns out it is true. There's more: his mother, who died recently at age 95, was one of the first female pilots in the world. It's on the Internet! 1928, the woman was a pilot—it's unbelievable! A friend of Amelia Earhart. I said, "How did your mother, a friend of Amelia Earhart, wind up marrying your father— who came to this country at age 13 and lived on the Lower East Side and sold newspapers to pay for food and lodging, before he went to Columbia and then became a physician? How did this happen?" Well, I'll tell you the story in a minute. This dinner was now number four of the remarkable events in my "day off."

I like to watch movies at night. That night: click, click, click . . . Most of them are junk; sometimes you hit a good one. This was on the *Sundance* channel— it's a mixed bag on *Sundance*. The movie this night: *Forty Shades of Blue*. What's it about? Well, it's a pretty amazing story. I was captivated: young, Russian girl, girlfriend of older record producer in Memphis, Tennessee, comes back to America. She's his live-in girlfriend. They have a child together but they're not married. He's played by Rip Torn as a garrulous, well-to-do guy down in the Memphis music industry. She's this stunning Russian beauty. They really love each other, apparently. Well, it's about her affair with his estranged son who comes to town for a party—it's a purely adult movie. It's something that many people would consider very slow, but if you like this kind of movie, it's like reading a novel—like a slow novel.

So, that was that. Then I had a little nightmare at night: maybe it was the lamb; maybe it was a mixture of the movie—I don't know. I've had the same, repetitive nightmare for 20 years, but that night it came back in spades. This time it was a box within a box. It was the same nightmare where I'm stranded in London, not able to get on a plane back to New York, and no matter how I try, I can't reach United Airlines, and there are no seats left. I have no hotel room—

every hotel is sold out in London. Virtually, I am homeless again, but this time, the dream was that I was awake telling everyone: "this is the dream I've been having, but it's really coming true."

I don't know why I had the dream: I have no idea. I don't know where this comes from or why, what triggers this whole dream sequence. That was my day, from morning till night: my "day off."

THERE IS A FLY IN THE STUDIO
and THE MIDGET
IN THE FLORIDA HOTEL

There is a fly in the studio. I'd like to kill it, but I'm the kind of guy who lets flies out of a window if I can. There's no window here, no screen. I want to just kill it with a newspaper. In two minutes you're going to hear me running after a fly. I hate flies; I hate them. They remind me of liberals. They always buzz around; they leave fecal matter everywhere; they supply nothing positive to the environment. They're always buzzing, buzzing, buzzing. A bee I don't mind as much as a fly. A bee doesn't bother me because I can see a bee—it doesn't weave and bob like a fly. A fly has a certain agility that a bee doesn't. Bees leave you alone by and large; a fly looks to bother you just because it can.

My father, may he rest in peace, taught me a trick. It's an old European trick. You take an undershirt off your body. You swing it overhead. You ever seen the old men do that, years ago? There're no old men around anymore. Where are the old men in this country? You never see them! When I grew up, there were old men around: old men, middle-aged men, young men. Today, everyone tries to look alike. With Viagra and hair transplants, it's like one continuum from age 15 till death. Everyone has dark hair, false teeth, and can be sexually aroused until they go into the coffin.

In my day, you got old and that was the end of it. They were old younger, though. The truth is, in my day, 40 was 60; 60 was 80—I don't know how it happened. In those days, they died younger: at 50, 55, a lot of them. Ever take a look at their diets? Smoked all day, didn't exercise, didn't take vitamins, never dieted. You can kill any good genetic inheritance with that kind of situation!

Have I told you the story of the thieving midget in the seedy hotel in Florida 25 years ago? He tried to rob me of my entire bankroll. I was a naïve kid from New York, and we took the Greyhound bus down to Florida. We couldn't even afford a $69 air ticket. It was like *Intercession*. It was like *Midnight Cowboy*. As we hit Atlanta there were chicken bones in the aisle. People were throwing food on the floor of the bus. It got so filthy! You really have to be a hero to use a Greyhound toilet. I would rather bust inside than—

Imagine going into a bus toilet in this day and age! Imagine what kind of needles are in there, or whatever. Even as a kid, I wouldn't use a bus toilet. A restroom in the back of the bus? Forget about it. It's toilet apartheid!

The best fried chicken I ever tasted in my life was in an Atlanta bus station. My mother tried to make fried chicken. It was OK, but I didn't like the oil; it didn't taste good. So I figure, *I'm in Atlanta at the bus stop Greyhound cafeteria,* so I decided to try the cuisine of the South in this place. What did I know? I was a kid from New York. I had no idea! *I figured, I'm in the South: I'm going to try Southern fried chicken.* Where am I going to try it? It was excellent! It was unbelievable! In those days, there was no KFC. They do a pretty good job, KFC—I've told you that—but this was better.

Maybe that's why I have a skin condition: not enough grease. Maybe I've cut down on the fats too much. Maybe if I had a high fat diet—you know, what if I went to a high cholesterol diet for a few days? I went and got the fish oil today: the Norwegian, the nitrogen-infused, $18 variety of cod liver oil—some special, hippie fish from Norway. They're all socialists. They're not racists. They're not homophobic fish! They danced in certain aquariums. And then they were harvested peacefully in their old age, and Dr. Death extracted their livers gently from his jail cell—and infused them with nitrogen.

I actually feel better from it, the fish liver oil. I grew up on it. Thank God I had fish liver oil as a child! I've got to tell you the truth: with the diet I ate, what my mother put into my mouth—you know how they force-feed a goose to make pâté? I was close to that in human form because my parents came from poverty in the Old World. See, they had a little money. The first thing they did was feed you. They didn't intend to give you a heart attack at 12!

But, it was a cardio-toxic diet. There's no question about it: ham & eggs for breakfast. Lunch was meatloaf from the night before, and at night you had a steak or pot roast, polished off with ice cream. Now, if you do that to an average human being today, they're dead at an early age.

Let's say you take Al Qaeda members and you say, "Here's your choice: we're either going to keep you in prison indefinitely with no charges for another 10 years or we will subject you to Michael Savage's childhood diet for three months, and if you don't get a heart attack, you're free." Know what I'm saying? It's a choice. Now, the reason I think I'm still alive is two-fold. A) I inherited the maternal side of the cardio-genetics, and B) it was the cod liver oil—because, despite the cardio-toxic diet, she gave me cod liver oil. She made me take it from a dropper bottle in orange juice. I hated it; I hated the taste of it. It was so disgusting!

To this day, it is remembrances of disgusting things past!

Drip, drip: "Take it, it's good for you." I hated it. "Take it or I'll kill you"—and the scissors came out, or the big kitchen knife in her eyes. Her eyes crossed and I knew I'd better take that orange juice. It was like getting a good mental wallop, you know, if I didn't take the juice. It was like the Kool-Aid: you look back on these things and it's lucky you didn't wind up in Guyana with Jim Jones. You know: "Take my Kool-Aid, man. Here are the drops in the Jell-O."

Caller-X is a guy I have not spoken to for 10 or 15 years, but he knows that the one-eyed midget from Miami story is 100 percent true.

SAVAGE: A.C., welcome to "The Savage Nation."

A.C.: Michael.

SAVAGE: I don't believe it. It's you! It really is you. I cannot believe it. I heard the other day that you are a listener.

A.C.: A guy called me and said, "You'd better call your buddy Mike Savage. He says you should call him." Some bartender called me, the very same guy from six to seven months ago. Mike, the big question is, remember how much money you put into the safe in Florida?

SAVAGE: No, how much? Wait. I'm going to guess: in those days, $35, my entire life savings.

A.C.: Bingo.

SAVAGE: No, are you serious? Was it 35 bucks?

A.C.: We put the money into the hotel safe in the morning; we came back at 6 o'clock—he didn't know what you were talking about!

SAVAGE: Was it not a bellhop midget?

A.C.: 23rd & Collins.

SAVAGE: 23rd & Collins. So that's South Beach today?

A.C.: You know, South Beach, they want to say, is below 21st Street. So it's not officially South Beach, but it's South Miami.

SAVAGE: Ok, but didn't the hotel beds have bed bugs?

A.C.: Of course.

SAVAGE: I woke up in the morning: I thought I was hallucinating. There were bed bugs in the hotel! Now, today I'll bet you that property is worth a pretty penny, no doubt.

A.C.: Mike, you don't remember: You went crazy with the guy! All of a sudden, he immediately—

SAVAGE: Wait. Let's slow down. We put the money in—all our money—in the safety deposit box in this flea-bag hotel. We come back: "I don't know about no money." I went crazy. Didn't we call for the police?

A.C.: We threatened to call for the police. The midget's eyes started rolling around in his head, the one eye, and all of a sudden, he remembered it was in the back safe.

SAVAGE: I pulled a loud yelling scene in the lobby.

A.C.: You went nuts.

SAVAGE: I gave him the command voice and the insanity—and the midget suddenly saw reality! He vaguely remembered the money. "Oh, I switched it to the other box," or something, right? It reappeared before the police arrived.

A.C.: It appeared, all of a sudden. He apologized profusely. What can I say? It was incredible.

SAVAGE: But see, people think I made up the "midget in the Miami hotel" story. Is it not true—and I won't get too personal—didn't you have an uncle who owned a hotel down there, a rich guy?

A.C.: You've got some memory.

SAVAGE: But wait, didn't he have a slight habit of stealing the sugar out of other hotels? I remember he owned a hotel, worth millions in those days—even in those days millions—but he had a habit: the sugar and the butter he took from other hotels.

A.C.: And the plastic spoons.

SAVAGE: That's right, because you never knew when you might need them, because he could be thrown out of Florida any minute!

A.C.: Michael, I have wanted to call you for the longest time. Are we on the radio now? Let me ask you this; there's one thing: where can I get Hakka Chinese cuisine here in the East Coast?

SAVAGE: Isn't that amazing? From the years you lived in San Francisco?

A.C.: You took me to the Hakka cuisine.

SAVAGE: Oh, yeah! You cannot get Hakka in New York? With that Chinese community, they never heard of it?

A.C.: All I know is that you turned me on to the greatest Chinese food in the world.

63

HANGOVER

I almost feel like moving away completely from the politics of the day which I've been talking about and going into what I did last night: the bars I drank in, the people I ran into—how I feel a little hung over today. I always do very good shows when I have a slight hangover. Not a very severe hangover, but a mild hangover is very, very good for radio, I find. I've always found it to be very good for radio—I don't know what it is. Let's see, what did I do last night?

So, as the curtain of night descended upon "The Savage Nation's" host, yours truly, Michael Savage, wandered up to the district known as North Beach in San Francisco, the more-or-less Italian district of the city. Actually, I didn't go directly there. I walked up. I have a certain walk I like that—I'm not going to tell you what it is because I don't want to be, let's say, accosted on the way—but, I walked through Chinatown on the way to North Beach because I love Chinatown. The reason I love to walk down Grant Avenue at night is because it gives me hope to see the small merchants closing their stores at night, raising their gates, securing their wares. It reminds me of my father's little store down in New York on Ludlow Street, how he would close the gates at night and lock it up and look, with love, at the merchandise that fed his family. Now, you don't see much of this anymore in America. Most of us are so removed from merchandise and being a shopkeeper.

In essence, the small businessman, the small businesswoman, is the core of the capitalist system and always has been, and probably always will be, despite the dominance of the great corporations. The small businessman is the key to the survival of a capitalist nation. Anyway, to make a long story short, I also like to see the Chinese people.

I like hearing, as I walk down the avenue, the young men, the vigorous young men, practicing martial arts in the upstairs studios, either through the drums—the drums are also part of the martial arts—I hear them practicing Tae Kwon-Do in some of the studios. I hear everything. As I walk, although my eyes are open, so are my ears. I have very sharp ears, and I listen to the sounds of the street. I don't have to know one word of Mandarin to understand what's going on. I say to myself, "You know, this gives me hope."

The reason it gives me hope is because I know that the Islamo-fascists will never conquer the Chinese, not in China nor in America. I said, "Are you kidding me? You're telling me these Chinese martial artists are going to let the Islamo-fascists dominate their neighborhood?" Never in a million years! That's all I can tell you. They have faced the conqueror in the past and they have driven the conqueror out. Of course there are times they've been conquered, if you want to get into the history of China and its conquest. The Muslims at a certain point conquered it, but I won't go into that because you don't know that half of China is Muslim—a good portion of China is Muslim as a result of conquest.

64

GARLIC AND JAZZ

In the U.S.A., I can tell you right now, most Chinese don't even know this is going on. These people live in their own world, and it's kind of nice to step into a world that is separated from my world. So, I walked through Chinatown, as I said, smelling the garbage in the street, and walked across Broadway. You step across Broadway and now you're suddenly stepping into the garlic world: the world of garlic and jazz, so to speak. You're in the Italian district.

For some reason I went to a place that I haven't been to for years. I used to hang out there a lot. It's an Irish bar. I looked for my friend because I hadn't seen him in years. We talked and I said, "How's your son?" He told me, "He's 10 years old." I haven't seen him in five years or more; I remember when he was a little boy in the bar.

I said, "You know, I still remember your Irish Wolfhounds. They're gigantic!" I watched his first Wolfhound grow up in the bar. I loved this dog. This dog was so big that his foot was bigger than my dog Teddy's entire body. One of the most beautiful dogs in the world—but he died at six.

I said, "You know, I remember your first dog." He said, "Oh, I had a second. He died, too. Now, I have a third, just a wee puppy." It was nice going in there. On the way in two guys offered to buy me a drink. I never accept a drink from a stranger, so I didn't accept the drink—but we got to talking. It turns out they're sheriff's deputies from another county in California, who just happened to hear my voice and say, "I can't believe our luck." And we talked, we talked about the fact that white men are being driven out of every sheriff's department, out of the highway patrol and every police department in the state of California, being replaced by lesbians, by Mexicans—being replaced by anyone but a white male.

65

RCA VICTOR DOG AT STORE; CONSTRUCTION AT STUDIO

A day in the life of a talk show host is ordinarily rather boring. So once in a while, I have to make sure it isn't boring. As I told you, I have several studios around the San Francisco Bay area. I shift around according to whim. So, I go into the city. I want to see people; I want to have lunch at my favorite greasy spoon Chinese restaurant so I can complain about the indigestion. I have a studio in an apartment building that was being renovated for over a year, wrecking everybody's life with jackhammers and smoke and noise. I figured that they were through with the scaffolding outside my balcony. I get there in the morning and sure enough, there was no scaffold outside my balcony. I said, "Alright, I picked a good day."

I stroll around town. I look at this and that, I go have lunch in my favorite Chinese greasy spoon. I ate the whole plate of chicken curry and got nauseous from it. I left, went out into the street like a dazed bumblebee who had been sprayed with Raid, the way I wanted to feel—because I didn't want to pay attention to the news.

I ambled over to an antique store, poked my head in—once in a while I enjoy it. I found an RCA Victor composition ceramic advertising "Dog Nipper," circa 1950, height 36 inches. I said, "What a great idea: I think I'll buy the RCA Victor dog." They wanted $1,295. I grew up in the antique business; I figured it was worth $5. If an upscale antique store is asking $1,295 it must be worth from $5 to $10, I figured. I figured I'd go back and look it up on Google.

Then, I found another thing I wanted: a mahogany decanter chest—remember those chests? When I was a little kid in my father's store, we would occasionally see these. I loved them. They were decanter chests with cut glass bottles that you'd put whiskey in and various beautiful glasses circa 1810. The price was $3,250. I wanted to buy it but I thought it was probably worth $250 on eBay. I put the brochures in my bag and headed up to the apartment with about an hour to go before the show. And, lo and behold, nightmare: the scaffolding is outside my deck again with jackhammers going, and smoke! I have to race up to the apartment, get my bag with stories, race down, jump in my car and race out of San Francisco, getting stuck behind every tourist on the road.

66

THE TIME SHELTER

I was recently on the streets of North Beach, the once-Italian district of San Francisco. Now it's the home to bums and Mainland China, with a remnant of Little Italy left: the Little Italy amusement park, North Beach. But thirty years ago when I came to San Francisco, there used to be women dressed in black—old, lean Italian women. They used to gossip with each other on the street, whispering. I loved it. Being the kind of guy I am, I would once in a while go up and talk to them. (Wherever I've been in the world, I've had the capacity to go up to strangers. I always get into good conversations for some reason.) I don't know how the conversation arose. I was talking to one of the old women—she must have been a good 95, probably Sicilian. I said to her, "Mama, what do you do for health?"

She says to me, "There's hardly anything wrong with a person that a little coffee, a little wine and a little garlic can't cure."

I agree with her 100 percent. Of course, I must add a few things to that mixture: Like, it's not a *little* wine; it's more than a little wine. It's not a *little* garlic; it's a lot more than a little garlic. And, there are other things that I like to do, but for her, it worked. They were beautiful old women. They're gone—you don't see them anymore.

I'm thinking of getting all 1950s items for a room—like a bomb shelter. I'll just call it a time shelter and go in it once a day to see the advertising dog, Jack Benny, Bob Hope, Dean Martin, Eisenhower, MacArthur, Einstein. Another time, another world.

67

CHEAP LABOR

A couple of years back I had an air conditioning system put into my house by a legitimate air conditioning firm, but I didn't know the workers he was using. Today I had an American air-conditioning man go in, a guy I know, to look at adding something for me. He said, "Do you know that your panel is burned out from what this guy put in? You could have burned your house down!" That's what we're talking about here: I had no idea he used a substandard electrician. I thought he used a union electrician. I had no way of checking!

CALLER: But that's what they're using. They're using nothing but illegal—

SAVAGE: Right. He got some guy who learned it in a trade school in Guadalajara, if that, or picked it up along the way. He didn't tell me that. He used somebody, some illegal alien—probably a relative—and put the money he saved into his own pocket. I didn't ask him to use a cheap electrician when he put the air conditioning in! So, this is what we're talking about.

See, I'm a lucky guy because I come from a blue-collar background—otherwise, I don't know what I'd be. It's very good to have your feet on the ground and know what reality is, and I don't know how a person who grew up living off the fat of the land, where everything is handed to them, can know what's really going on down at the street level. I guess I'm very lucky in a way that my father was so gruff to me. I didn't want to do what he made me do; to me it seemed mean, but he was right in a way. We fought like crazy, but I'll never forget the day he dragged me out of that house and said, "That's it: you're going to work."

So, I went from this spoiled little world down into a basement in his store, where I had to work like a bum, cleaning bronze statutes with a cyanide solution. I've told the story already. The point I'm making is that I resented it, but in a way,

I learned about labor—horrible labor, disgusting work—and I was able to do it. I've got to tell you something: once you're trained to work, once you're committed to being a worker, you can't stop. There's no retirement. What do you mean, retirement? I don't even know what the word means! I'm an inner-city kid. I'm not proud of it, I'm just not *un*proud of it.

As I've said before, I never learned to play tennis. I never learned to play golf. I know friends who grew up in the same world as I did who, early on, took up tennis and golf—and if that's what they want, fine! I never found it interesting. I'd rather roll on the rug and play with my dog and stick my fingers in his mouth and pull on his canine teeth than play golf. But, if you like it, God bless you.

The point is a little different. When I went to college, skiing was just becoming big, and some of the guys I grew up with took up skiing in Vermont. I got the ski pants but never took up skiing. I liked the outfit. I thought that they would attract girls, so I got ski pants—and, they worked! I've got to tell you the truth: in those days it was before I could afford to eat a lot so, consequently, the ski pants had their benefits. But, I never took up skiing.

As a kid, though, I learned how to use a sled. It was fun to go downhill in the Bronx. I almost got killed under a truck. To this day I can remember the truck. Can you imagine I grew up in a time when trucks had chain drives on them? Monster trucks that had chains going around their wheels!

So, a kid's uncle took the three of us on a sled. The uncle must have been 20, but to me he was an old man. All three of us bellied up on a sled: an American Flyer, I think—who knows what it was. And so we're shooting down a hill and he lost control of the sled. I swear to God that it went under the truck as it was moving—I thought we were going to be crushed!—and shot out on the other side of the truck. It shows you what kids go through: they can die by accident for no reason whatsoever.

But, I've worked. I've worked minimum wage jobs. I worked in an ice cream factory: horrible, disgusting summer job, putting ice cream bars inside boxes. I was on a line in a factory. Did you ever work in a factory? Well, don't talk about minimum wage unless you have. You try putting 24 bars of frozen ice cream inside a box as it comes by you in about x-number of seconds!

My friend's father owned the ice cream factory; didn't do me any good. They put me on the production line. So, you had to fill the box. The boxes are coming around—I don't know how many seconds you had to stuff them in; five seconds, let's say. If you missed your 24 bars in that box, the foreman stopped the line. The overseer would hit a button and yell out, "You moron idiot you! Look what you made me do, you stupid moron!"

Today, teachers take the morons and put them in front of the class and tell you that the moron is smarter than you are—and the smart kid has to hide his smartness because we're living in a Communistic America. This is a Communist system we have developed in this great country of ours! "Don't play tag, you're liable to make children feel inferior." "Don't do this, don't do that," and that's why we're a nation of losers.

68

UNSUCCESSFUL PEOPLE

I was thinking about some of the unsuccessful people that I've known and why they're unsuccessful. I've been thinking about it because for many years I struggled in life. It wasn't that I wasn't trying: I wrote a lot of books. I made a reasonable living, but it wasn't what I wanted, in terms of success. It was a grind—it was a real grind. I realized something: there were people all the way up and down the scale, way beyond me and way below me, but I realized that there's a whole class of unsuccessful people in the world. Let's focus on the people you know who have never really made it in life: I asked myself, "What do unsuccessful people have in common?"

I wrote a few notes down—tell me if you agree or disagree. Unsuccessful people have an unwillingness to give of themselves, or to offer a product or service that people want. Now I have to add "that people want" because many of you out there have offered products or services that people do not want. They may want it in the future—you can be ahead of your time. You could be a genius. (Most likely you're not a genius, you're just a person who's producing things that nobody wants, but I will say that there are many cases where people were ahead of their time and they did produce great inventions that nobody wanted at the time.) But, by and large, unsuccessful people are unwilling to give of themselves or to offer a product or service that people want.

Let me give you a political example: politicians offer products that are grossly unpopular. What are these products? Higher taxes. Affirmative action. Gay marriage. Wars. I'm giving you four examples. These are the products that politicians offer that are grossly unpopular. But because the people don't want them, the politicians still try to force society to "buy them" by forcing you to take them through legislation. That's called "judge shopping" or "activist judges." That's how they force gay marriage, affirmative action, higher taxes, and illegal wars down our throat. So in other words, politicians are offering products that are grotesquely unpopular but they force them on us.

But to return to unsuccessful people, per se, they generally see kindness as weakness and only want to take from others. Only grudgingly do they ever offer a kind word or deed to others. Now this applies to societies as well. For example, our country, the United States of America, was, until recently, the world's most successful society. We're also the most giving society on earth. According to the liberal protocols, we're not a successful society and we don't give much. It's a complete lie! This is the most successful society in terms of the broadest good for the broadest number of people, and it is the most giving in the entire world. That's why we're successful.

But, to go back to unsuccessful people. Now there are people who cannot produce a product or a service that people want—I understand that—so let's say they're on the receiving end. They receive gifts or grants from foundations and only grudgingly say "thank you" to the foundation that gave them the money. In other words, they don't even go out of their way to cultivate the foundation, and then they wonder why the grant doesn't get renewed!

Or, let's say they're given a gift from a relative, that the relative doesn't owe them. Instead of saying "thank you" in a profound way—real gratitude—they are grudging in thanking the people who gave them the money. So the relative says, "You know what, screw you. I don't owe you anything. Why should I give you anything?" Then, the money runs out and the unsuccessful person says, "Oh, woe is me! I wonder why people are so mean in this world."

Do you agree with me that unsuccessful people generally are unwilling to give of themselves or to offer a product or service that people want? I think it's an interesting question.

69

LIFE FROM
A CHILD'S PERSPECTIVE

SAVAGE to **CALLER (PAUL)**: You're asking me to tell you what I think about perceptions of reality, the difference between the perceptions of reality of a child and an adult, or a child and an old person?

PAUL: You made an observation and I made the same observation, where— I think you were studying on your boat—you said it kind of hit you that when you were a child, everything kind of had a grand, big, bigger-than-life kind of feel to it. Then, when you got—maybe, like I'm in my 30s, where everything becomes mundane, and—

SAVAGE: Oh! How a child sees the world! Well, I have a dog that has to substitute for a child, and so his perceptions are different than a child's, but you know, when you watch a dog react to things you will notice every sound is bigger than life, and it's the same for a child. To a child, it's all brand new. Can you imagine what a rainbow must look like to a child? As we get older, rainbows still inspire most of us but we're somewhat jaded. I think that's what you're referring to, that kind of gross interpretation.

PAUL: It is, but you said the observation was that as you got older you started to get some of that back. You start to 'smell the roses,' again.

SAVAGE: Could have been I had enough B_3 that day—I don't really know. I don't have any explanation. It could have been the Niacin.

PAUL: But that is right in line with Einstein's Special Theory of Relativity, where he—

SAVAGE: How so? What does he say?

PAUL: He basically boils it down to stating that time is relative. It's relative to the perspective of the person watching the train versus the person on the train.

SAVAGE: There's another analogy that my friend, a physicist, repeated on radio last week. He said it's like the issue of monkeys on a typewriter: monkeys are dancing on the keys of a typewriter, and letters are typed. People think that monkeys are typing the letter, but in fact, they're just randomly dancing on the keys of a typewriter. Does that more or less fit?

PAUL: I'm not really sure if that's what I'm trying to convey.

SAVAGE: Let's take the analogy of monkeys dancing on keys of a typewriter. That would be the newspeople today, the journalists. Because they're typing letters that are somewhat literate, meaning they're spelled correctly and they make sentences, they think that they're writing the news. But it has no relationship to what the news really is! Let's go back to Plato, where Plato said, "Most of us don't see reality. We only see the shadows on the wall." Does that work for you?

PAUL: That's closer. Like I said, it was an explanation, an observation that you made. I do remember being a child; I do remember every once in a while—

SAVAGE: Or are you saying that, because I said that you were able to relate back to being a child yourself, and remember what it was like to be a child? I think most of us—occasionally, when we're super-relaxed and we're really in a state of calm—we can sometimes look back and, for a moment, see that way again. That is called inner peace.

70

BEING DECENT IS NOT LOVE

If you are decent to others, then you're decent to yourself. You feel better. I don't want to say if you love others, you love yourself, because I think the word "love" is over-used—and it's not the right verb anyway. I've told you that. In Latin there are 16 verbs for love. We have one verb for love and we get mixed up: I love my girlfriend, I love my mother, I love my pizza, I love my bike, I love my car, and I love my dog. In the Latin there are 16 different verbs for these emotions.

Here, we're so limited by the choice of the one verb "love" that we mix up a pizza with our mother and our girlfriend and our bicycle! That's why I avoid the word "love" altogether—I don't like it. It makes me uncomfortable. You love me? You love me, honey? Everything in America is "love."

I'm an Old World kind of guy. I was raised with it. My father never believed in the word love. He got mad if you said "love" around him. He knew it was B.S. "I love everybody." You can't love strangers that you don't know, but you can be nice to them. You don't have to go out of your way to be a fool.

My line is: if you are decent to other people, you're decent to yourself. You feel better. Try it for a day. Look, let's say you're a typical, mean S.O.B. You cut people off, you give them the finger, you're an obnoxious, cheap, hateful human being—the average American in other words. Try one day to be decent to strangers. See the power of human kindness.

71

MAN IS A CREATURE
OF REASON

I was reading the teachings of Buddha, called *The Way of Practical Attainment*. Here's one; tell me whether this applies to you. It doesn't matter what your religion is. Listen to this:

"A man who chases after fame and wealth and love affairs is like a child who licks honey from the blade of a knife: while he is tasting the sweetness of honey he has to risk hurting his tongue. He is like a man who carries a torch against the strong wind: the flame will surely burn his hands and face. People love their egoistic comfort, which is a love of fame and praise, but fame and praise are like incense that consumes itself and soon disappears. If people chase after honors and public acclaim and leave the way of truth, they're in serious danger and will soon have cause for regret."

It's beautiful poetry, I've got to tell you that. It's universal in the sense that it crosses over to whatever your religion might be. Even if you're an atheist you can find these rules somewhat reasonable to live by, unless you don't believe in any rules at all because you're so wild and free. Oh, we understand that—we understand that people who aren't religious are just "wild and free" and they're so progressive in their freedom and their liberation. As George Orwell said, "The more people chant about their freedom and how free they are, the more loudly I hear their chains rattling."

"A scripture that is not read with sincerity soon becomes covered with dust." Who does that sound like? You remember the staged Bibles of the Clintons? Remember that overly large Bible they used to carry on Sundays, that was made for them in Hollywood, on a Hollywood set? It was one and a half to two and one-half times the size of an ordinary Bible. The cross was so big you couldn't miss it from 100 yards away! "A scripture that is not read with sincerity soon becomes covered with dust." "A house that is not fixed when it needs repairing becomes filthy; so an idle man soon becomes defiled."

Why do you think each nation, each people, and each religion, has these writings? What is the purpose of any of this? If you were just left to your wants and to your needs and what you're moaning about—"Oh, I don't have this, I don't have that. I don't have an airplane. Oh, I don't have a girlfriend. Oh, I don't have 10 girlfriends. Oh, I don't have a house in Aspen next to Diane Feinstein, the war profiteer. Oh, I'm not him. Oh, I'm not invited there."—you're going to just moan and groan through your whole life!

You have to understand that there are millions, tens of millions of people like you on the earth, going through exactly the same moanings and groanings and that you have to find your way out of it without taking a pill, without dosing yourself up on a bicycle ride. There's nothing wrong with taking a pill if you need it, or taking a bicycle ride—trust me on that one—but that's not the point. That shouldn't be your only way out of a problem. If man is anything, he is a creature of reason. Do you understand what I'm saying to you? How do you define man? Man is an animal who reasons.

Let's say you don't believe in God, our Creator, so you're into mechanism. You say, "Well, we're only animals." We have animal bodies, but you have to admit that we are animals who reason. So, therefore, if a man reasons—or a man *can* reason—then he can think his way out of almost any problem that he puts himself in. All these problems, by the way, are temporal—small problems, these wants and these needs. If you thought yourself into them, you should be able to think your way out of most of them.

But, you can't do it all on your own. Some of them you could try on your own, but you're probably not going to be able to succeed. See, that's when people start to turn to the Scriptures or to the teachings of Buddha or to another religion—Zen Buddhism, or yoga.

To me it all looks like a burlesque when I look into a yoga studio: I feel like I'm from another planet. If you're doing yoga, why do you have to wear a costume that shows your private parts to everyone in the room? Can't you do yoga wearing something that's a little more dignified, I ask myself? I mean, if it's purely for the spirit, to get control of the spirit, why are they wearing a show-all pair of tights and they're on their hands and knees? I just ask myself if it's what they say it is!

See, you have to find the answer somewhere else than in your own head. In other words, we are creatures, we are animals that reason, so we can use reason to get out of any hole that we find ourselves in. But, we don't have to write the scriptures to get us out of that hole. Let's go to the people who thought this through 10,000 years ago, 5,000 years ago, 1,000 years ago. We don't need some "author" who was on Oprah to get us out of it! He probably stole it from one of these books anyway and re-packaged it! You may as well go back to the original guys who wrote the stuff.

"To conquer oneself is a greater victory than conquering thousands in a battle." Think about that one; I can never understand that one. If a man's pointing a gun at you—or, if a man wants to do you harm, let's put it to you that way—I really don't have time for that one. I still sleep with the doors locked and the alarm on and the guns loaded, with the dogs at my side. I don't trust that much in it, this saying.

Here's the last one of this preachy stuff today. This is from the teaching of Buddha, and the reason I'm reading it is not because I'm a Buddhist but because the poor people of Burma are. And so, here's another one of the practical guides that perhaps one of them read: "The duty of a ruler is to protect his people." How's that for a starter, Mr. Bush? "The duty of a ruler is to protect his people," and many of us would say he is. OK. "He is the parent of his people and he protects them by his laws." Well, when Bush says, "childrens do learn" we start to wonder what kind of parent he might be.

The Buddhist teaching goes on:

"He must raise his people like parents raise their children, giving a dry cloth to replace a wet one without waiting for the child to cry. In like manner, the ruler must remove suffering and bestow happiness without waiting for people to complain. Indeed, his ruling is not perfect until his people abide in peace. They are his country's treasure."

I love that one: the people are a nation's treasure. You hear what I'm saying to you? We are the treasure of America! You and I are the treasure of America: not the senators, not the congressmen, not the media pimps. We are the treasure of America!

"Therefore a wise ruler is always thinking of his people and does not forget them even for a moment." Wouldn't you like to believe that? Wouldn't you like to wake up or go to sleep knowing that your wise rulers are always thinking of you and don't forget you for a moment other than to deceive you and to fleece you?

"He thinks of their hardships and plans for their prosperity. To rule wisely, he must be advised about everything: about water, about drought, about storms, about rain. He must know about crops, the chances for a good harvest, people's comforts and their sorrows. To be in a position to rightly award, punish, or praise, he must be thoroughly informed as to the guilt of bad men and the merits of good men."

It's an interesting thing about rulers in here. I don't want to read anymore because I think you've got the picture. That's why I've touched on various religious writings. When you hear these people say they're the wrong gender trapped in a body, for example—the current psychosis among the transgender crowd—he's a woman trapped in a man's body so he's going to go to a surgeon to cut off his penis. To me, that's total insanity! The doctor should be arrested for malpractice, and the person who thinks that about himself should be given anti-psychotic medication or put into a mental ward.

Never before in history has a man awakened and said, "I'm a woman in a man's body." Never! This is propaganda. There may have been homosexuals on earth from the beginning of time and there may be homosexuals on earth till the end of time—we understand that—but to say you're a woman in a man's body— can't you just be a man who likes men? Why must you say you're a woman in a man's body? Where'd that come from? That comes from the psychosis of the psychiatric movement that has convinced thousands of marginally sane people that they're men born in women's bodies!

But just as I can read Buddhist scripture and I don't have to be a Buddhist, I don't have to say I'm a Buddhist trapped in an American's body. I don't have to become a Buddhist to read the Buddhist tracts. You don't have to shift religions just to read the other religion's books. You don't have to say, "Now I'm trapped in the wrong religion." You were born in a religion. That's the religion that's right for you. It's genetic! It's part of your genetic code. Your parents were that religion. Going back to however many generations, was that your religion? It's in your genetic code. It's encoded within your mind and your psyche—and you're never going to find peace in another religion! Never. Never! You're always going to be confused. You may find temporary peace by saying, "Oh, I'm a Buddhist." Stop trying to change religions, jumping from one to another like you'd jump between hobbies.

Have you ever seen these liberal American "Buddhists" walking around? They don't even know what Buddhism means! They use it as a form of ego pride. They're trying to show they're different than you, better than you—that they've evolved from, let's say, Catholicism into Buddhism.

Now the first teaching of Buddhism will tell you that you can't use a religion as a matter of pride, as the Iranian Hitler did. He used his religion as a matter of pride. He was misusing his own religion by bashing us over the head with it and saying, "The world will not be peaceful until you all accept my religion." To me, that's the mark of a person who doesn't even understand his own religion. You can't misuse your religious book and say, "You must be like *me,* you must follow *my* religion, or there will be no peace on earth!" You're abusing your religious teachings! It's the opposite of your religion to do that!

But nobody said that to Iran's Hitler. Bush had the chance to do that in the United Nations. He's our leader; he could have gotten up there and said 10 things we would have remembered. He could have had somebody write a speech for him that said, "We have a visitor to America today, who is using his religion in a prideful manner, trying to tell us that unless we convert to his religion there will be no peace on earth. This is the act of a lowly man who is hostile to the rest of the world, and it has no place in the United Nations, where humanism and humanitarianism should prevail—not threats." He could have said that. The world would have stood up and cheered and said, "What got into him? Who wrote that speech for him?" (Who is Bush's speechwriter, by the way? What has happened to the speech-writing profession? Have they all become Webmasters and bloggers? Where are they? Does anyone write for this guy?)

Here's a recent Bush speech. I would like to know who wrote this one for him: "As yesterday's positive report card shows, childrens do learn when standards are high—." Childrens do learn. He's lecturing children in America on education and he says, "Childrens do learn."

You can laugh at it and say he gets tongue-tied—I'm sorry, he's the president of the United States! Communication skills are essential to be a president. If a president can't communicate, what can he do? It's not funny anymore; it's an embarrassment. It's embarrassing to listen to this!

And that's part of the problem. It goes back to this core statement: that national pride has never been this low in my lifetime. I've never seen national pride at this low point. We are at the lowest point of national pride that I can ever remember. Tell me if I'm wrong: can you remember a day that national pride was lower than it is today? On September 12th, 2001, it was higher than it is today! The day after the Islamic murderers hit us, the nation was very proud because we knew we were going to fight back and we were going to beat them—but we haven't beaten them for all the cowardly reasons that we know to be in play.

But, we were proud to be Americans that day. We all came together. We were prouder the day *after* we were hit than we are today. We have a leader who is not articulate; we have an opposition party that is simply mean-spirited and grubby. All they want to do is take as much money from the nation's treasury as they can with "earmarks," and we, the people—who are the true pride of the nation and the true treasure of the nation—are left without anyone at the helm! Who is at the helm? There is no helm at all. And that's where we sit today.

72

TALKING TO A BUM ABOUT GOD

I don't know how many houses of worship I've tried in my life that I've walked out of. I walked out of them sometimes because I was bored, sometimes because I thought their politics were too far to the Left. I've walked out of many houses of worship. In fact, I never found one that I liked. And yet, I'm a man who believes in God. Why? Who am I *not* to believe in God? Who am I to say, "I don't believe in God"? What do you think I am: bigger than God? "I created myself," a man once said to me. "Follow your logic in your own head," a homeless man said to me.

I was once into, more so than now, talking to strangers. I was the wandering man who would talk to weird people, figuring they held the truth, or some truth. Now I hold my own truths. I don't need to talk to strangers to form my opinions. I can come up with my own, but when I was younger, I talked to a lot of odd people. One of them was an itinerant man. You'd call him a bum, but he wasn't really because he wasn't really dirty. He wasn't disheveled; he didn't look like a homeless man, but he was. He had a backpack and long white hair. He wasn't particularly clean and he wasn't particularly dirty, and he wasn't an alcoholic or a druggie. So, I talked to him about this and that.

His name was Morris (or Moses). So, I said to him, "Do you believe in God?" I remember to this day—it was on Columbus Avenue in San Francisco. I looked at him and he had startling blue eyes. He looked at me and said, as though in astonishment, "Why? Who created you?" In that instant, I had a *satori*, like the Japanese talk about. I understood more completely than I ever had through any preacher or rabbi what it was all about.

Follow it back: "Do you believe in God?," I say to the itinerant man.

He says, stunned, "Why? Who created you?"

I got it in that flash—you know, that flash of understanding; the *satori?*

Follow it back. So you're an atheist and you say, "Well, how do you know there's a God?" So what is there, nothing? So nothing created you? So you believe in nothing? Therefore, you believe in something—but that's nothing. You believe in nothingness.

I believe in God. That's all. How can you believe in nothingness? How is it possible to believe in nothingness? How can something come from nothing? It's a violation of all the laws of physics! Something cannot come from nothing. It violates physical science, biological science, theological science. It violates all the laws of reason! It violates all the laws of non-reason. So, what I'm getting at is what I learned from that man.

So then I said, "Can I drop you off where you're going?" (I had my Volkswagen at the time.) I drove him to a freeway overpass that no longer exists. The man got out and said goodbye. He disappeared, and I never saw him again. Who was he? A prophet? Was he a reincarnation of a religious figure? I don't know what he was. Maybe he was just a smart guy who was a bum. A lot of bums are smart, and a lot of corporate guys are not that smart. They play people for fools. They think that everybody is a fool because they control the money.

What they don't understand is that there are values beyond money. They've never learned that. Unfortunately, our government is exactly the same. It's MBA all the way, right up into the military hierarchy. They think that an MBA makes them a war hero or a sage, but many would take a pound of flesh or sell their country out for less than 30 pieces of silver. They would teach their children Chinese and move to Shanghai if they had a better offer! Not me, buddy. For me the "bottom line" is God, not dollars.

73

MAMA SAVAGE
IN A RETIREMENT HOME
AND HER FOOD

SAVAGE: Dallas, Texas: Devon, you're on "The Savage Nation." Topic please?

DEVON: I want to hear the story about your mother when she was, I believe, living in a retirement home and she complained about the food, and she wanted to have special food brought in. And you found out later that the food was great and she was just trying to put a guilt trip on you.

SAVAGE: You remember the story better than I do. She got bored in the nursing home—whatever they call it, "assisted living." In my day it was called an "old-age home," but now they call it "assisted living."

Alright, so she's in the home. It was a lovely place in Florida. It was, in reality, an "8." Food was perfectly fine, but she was a woman who liked her own food in her own ways.

So I'd call from where I was living in California, "Mom, what can I do to help you?"

"Can you get me Chinese food, or Italian?" That's all she said toward the end.

So, I went through contortions. I called a local Chinese place. I said, "Well, Ma, can't you just call a Chinese place and have them deliver and put it on my credit card?"

"No," she said, "they don't deliver."

"Well," I said, "Call an Italian joint down there in Del Ray. They'll deliver."

"No, no one delivers."

I went through machinations. I called a taxi company; I got a nice guy, Jake.

He said, "Yeah, I'll do it for your mother. I don't know who you are but you sound like a nice guy. I'll drive; I'll get the food."

I said, "Alright, charge me the cab fare plus $15." I did this for weeks: I had Chinese and Italian delivered.

Weeks later I found out that the assisted living facility had food delivered from the same restaurants! She was doing it just to work me over, God bless her—another guilt trip. Look, they're like children in the end. Just imagine what I'll be like if I'm lucky enough to live that long. But I don't think anyone will take care of me the way I did my mother. I think I'm more like my father. I don't know how long I want to live or how long I will live. It's really not in my hands. Up to a certain point it is, but I'm nowhere near that, although sometimes I'm thinking of checking into an assisted living facility, for one reason.

See, the radio business is very lonely. You're alone 99 percent of the time. Then you're on the radio like a nut, talking into a microphone. In a "home" it wouldn't be bad. You can argue over things there; you get up at five in the morning; there's always a coffee pot. There are people to like, there are people to hate. You know, when she was in that home, the assisted living place, it was very nice. Next to her was a man 50 years old, a doctor. Would you believe that he lost his mind? He was in there at 50: a big guy; he was frightening looking. Every time I came in he was like a Frankenstein, looming. Something happened. His mind went on him, and they wound up putting him in this joint. I was afraid he would kill her! He never hurt a fly, but I feared that one day he'd pick up a cleaver and kill everyone in the home.

There were men as young as 50 in some of these places that—to the outside eye, to the unaided eye—looked perfectly normal. But I don't know: they checked in there. There's nothing to do in those places. And as you start to deteriorate, they move you up in floors. If you're on floor three, you're still good—two and three. Four: already you're going in the head. Five: already you're babbling. And six: you're in the Alzheimer's ward; there's nothing left upstairs. So, the fear was to be moved up by floors. My mother used to say, "I'm not going up . . . ."

74

NO ASSISTED LIVING

I don't look for them but once in a while I get a call like this: "Dr. Savage, maybe you can help me. I haven't gone to the toilet very well in the last few weeks. Since Thanksgiving I've had a blockage. Can you give me . . . ."

Or I might get another one. "Is there something natural I could use because my wife and I are no longer doing the funny business together? I don't want to use that stuff that makes your vision turn blue with mild blindness."

I told you one of the side affects of Viagra is temporary blindness in some men. I jokingly said that's part of the effect that's desired: that's why you can still do it with someone you've lived with for so many years. It makes you temporarily blind, and that's it. You put the blinders on instead of taking them off—not so funny.

The poor women, what they have to put up with! No wonder the men die first! After putting up with us for so long, they're supposed to get it all in the end. I don't know what they do with it, frankly; I don't know if they enjoy themselves. They seem to enjoy themselves, the older women, and here's why: A) Their sex drives have left them, and they're not bothered with that. B) They could do without men. They find out that it was all a myth to begin with. They had the children already, the grandchildren. What do they need men for at a certain point? They've got some money; they can travel.

What do they do in the "old age" homes? I know I'm never going to wind up in assisted living or an old-age home. Never. I know I'm never going to be there! My mother wound up in assisted living. I told you—it was only about Italian or Chinese food for her. That's all that she would talk about.

I would say, "Mom, my latest book is a best-seller for the 15th week on the *New York Times'* Bestseller List."

She'd say, "That's nice. You know, I had Italian last night. It wasn't so good. It wasn't as good as in New York." That's all! I'd get that repeatedly.

I have figured this out. No homes for me if I should live long—or longer. Tick, tock, tick, tock. I'm watching the sands of time fall into the hourglass. There's more sand down on the bottom now than there is on the top. You know what I'm saying? If you take the hourglass of your life when you're a certain age, there's more sand up above in that glass than there is down below. In my case, most of the sand has already gone down to the bottom glass. I'm starting to think about certain things I have ignored up until now.

People say to me, even today, "What do you want to do at the end?"

I say, "I'm never going to die." They think I'm crazy. I won't make such plans. I will *not* make such plans. I'm never going to die. I'm never going to get sick! How do you like that? In other words, you say I'm foolish. Alright. Call it what you want.

I knew kids when I lived in Hawaii, mainly Japanese-Americans, and at 19 years old they knew whom they were going to marry. They knew where they were going to get married, how many children they were going to have. They knew where they were going to be buried. At 19 they had it all worked out!

There are societies that do that to this day. I don't understand that kind of living. I can't do that! I'd rather live with the sensibilities of a man who's going to live a thousand years! I remember that character out of *Zorba*—do you remember Kazantzaki's great character Zorba the Greek? I love that character. Of course, it was a distortion. It was played by Anthony Quinn. Do you remember this scene? He's leaning against a window and says to a woman, "A man like me should live 1,000 years." What a great line that is! That's the way to go through life every day, by the way.

I don't like men who, at 50, say, "Well, at my age," or "I'm 50 and I think I've already got one foot in the grave." Why think that way? Why start taking that attitude? You're just going to speed up your own aging and die young if you think that way! Even if, let's say, I should become enfeebled by accident or disease, I'm never going to go into assisted living. I want to stay in the house, and I want to have care—that's all! I don't want to be around a hospital: the other people smell like piss and mothballs in those joints. There's no reason to be there. You get around-the-clock care if you can. I'll make sure that I put it away for that. Another car? I'd rather pay for care.

192

75

SAVAGE FOR PRESIDENT

SAVAGE: Peter, make it succinct, thank you. What's on your mind?

PETER: Yes, Dr. Savage, it's a pleasure talking to you. I just want to say that I'm a Vietnam veteran and I can't wait—at 6:06 when you come on, I just can't wait for that time to come. Your destiny is for president of the United States. That's the only destiny I see in this land! You are the salvation of America, and Dr. Savage, you have to do it. I don't know how you're going to do it, but you've got my—

SAVAGE: Peter, I know this. I know that your sincerity is heartfelt. On my Web site I think we have over 75 million people who have gone and said, "Mike, leave radio. Run for office." I can't believe the numbers! We passed the 75 million mark. I don't know how accurate this is, but I'll tell you right now, it's in the many millions, Peter—that's the number of people who are fed up with the two-party system. They know that they're both cons. But you know, Peter, haven't we seen in this election that without money, you can't get anywhere in this country? Haven't we seen that the system is bought and sold for so many pieces of silver—perhaps 30 pieces of silver, if you get the meaning, Peter? Peter, how do you run against a machine where a guy like Barack Obama—an unknown man with no credit to his name, no known books to his name other than a fabricated book about his life, with no history of having achieved one bill of any significance—can attract crowds of 75,000? The answer is: money, money, money; brainwashing and power.

If you're a Vietnam vet you know something about the history of the world because you fought the Communists. You realize that the propaganda minister for Adolph Hitler, whose name was Joseph Goebbels, said the following, "If you tell a big lie often enough, it will become the truth."

So, if you tell the big lie that Obama is the savior over and over and that no matter how big a lie it was at first, the propaganda machine is daily. The gullible, weak-minded people start to believe it. Just as with the myth of global warming, if you tell that big lie over and over and over again, people start to believe it.

Remember, in the beginning the Germans didn't particularly love the Jews. They didn't particularly hate the Jews, but the big lie machine started saying, "Jews are this, Jews are that. Jews did this, Jews did that." And it was everyday. It was like a drip of water on the mind, on the consciousness of the German people, until eventually enough Germans started to believe it was true.

Peter, we're living through the greatest propagandist time in the history of this country. The media is pushing this unknown man; the media is pushing the myth of global warming; the media is pushing the lie that all immigrants come here to work; the media is pushing the myth that two homosexuals should get married. The media is pushing one myth after another, Peter, and they're destroying the public mind. Do you understand that?

PETER: But you have to understand that you are the only salvation for us!

SAVAGE: Peter, listen to me. I don't need to be president to be your salvation. Listen to me, God is not the president of the United States, is he? But he's your salvation. Anyone who picks up a Bible has salvation, and God is eternal. He doesn't have to run for office! He doesn't need to be a congressman or a senator. His words are in the Bible! My words are on the radio and my words are in my books—that's where I live. I don't want to be part of a corrupt, broken machine.

Afterword:
The Autism Storm

T he real cases of autism deserve our sympathy and our financial support. It is the misdiagnosed, the falsely diagnosed, and the profiteers I would like to address.

Let me get very personal: I had a severely disabled brother who suffered and died in a New York snake pit of a mental hospital. I know first-hand what true disability is. To permit greedy doctors and drug companies to include children in medical categories that may not be appropriate is a crime against those children and their families. Let the truly autistic be treated; let the falsely diagnosed be free.

There *are* children who are genuinely autistic, and of course they need as much love and attention and help as we can give them. However, many children are being victimized as doctors misdiagnose them; they may not be autistic at all. Did you know that the American Academy of Pediatrics recently recommended dangerous anti-cholesterol drugs for children as young as two years of age? Without any scientific studies on the possible dangers of such drugs on children, corrupt doctors made this controversial, unscientific recommendation: "Give children as young as two years old anti-cholesterol drugs."

Why is this happening? It is happening increasingly because our children are being used as profit centers by a greedy, corrupt medical/pharmaceutical establishment.

I thought about my poor, deceased brother, who lived without having spoken a word his entire life. He lived into his twenties. He was given away when he was very young—five or six. It tore the family to pieces. He was sent to a snake pit on

Staten Island where he suffered for 20 years. He died in that hospital, never having spoken a word. I thought, *Should I bring up the memory of my brother? Is it cruel to do this? Should I use him to defend me?* Then you know what came to me? I thought, *Yeah, I'm going to tell the story of Jerome. Maybe my defenseless brother, who never spoke a word, can speak boldly in defense of his brother 50 years later. And then the power of the silent brother will be heard.* So I've told that story, and now I want to talk about the issue that story hits on, an issue I've been immersed in over the past several years.

Interview with Dr. Peter Breggin, Psychiatrist:

Years ago Dr. Peter Breggin, a psychiatrist, was on my radio program, warning America about the dangers of over-diagnosis of ADD and ADHD and particularly, the drugging of our children with Ritalin. I recently asked Dr. Breggin, "Do you know much about this new epidemic, the number of newly-diagnosed people with autism?

DR. BREGGIN: I think it's a continuing marketing effort. The drug companies have really saturated America with drugs, so they are constantly pushing to expand the diagnoses. They have tried everything from drugging sub-clinical conditions—that is, conditions that don't even meet the regular clinician's eye—to using all the adult drugs with children (which is a disaster), and spreading it to so-called bi-polar disorder or manic depressive disorder in children. I have never personally seen that in children, except when psychiatric drugs cause it. Finally, this broadening of the concept of autism to autism spectrum disorders (ASD)—almost all of the experts, Michael, who are involved in this spreading of the diagnostic categories are in the pay of the drug companies.

SAVAGE: Unbelievable! You know, it's been very hard on me, being attacked for telling the truth. We had an expert on yesterday, Dr. Stephen Camarata of Vanderbilt University, who is an autism expert and treats it regularly. He actually said that about 58 percent of the cases are falsely or misdiagnosed—even he admits that! You go a step further. What percent would you say are not autistic?

DR. BREGGIN: Well, I think the diagnoses do more harm than good in general. I avoid diagnosing children with psychiatric disorders because it labels them; it puts them into boxes, encourages the use of psychiatric drugs. I try to understand what is happening in the child's life. A lot of children who are labeled autistic are simply greatly in need of socialization, of a lot more attention from parents and teachers and counselors. So as far as I'm concerned, it's not a good idea to go around diagnosing kids—or drugging them.

Now we do, of course, have the reality of children who, at an early age, failed to relate in a normal fashion to their moms and dads and the people around them. Most of these children, if you look at them and watch their behavior, they actually don't relate to people as if they're people.

SAVAGE: Wait—let's go back. Now first, Dr. Breggin, you're a psychiatrist; is that correct?

DR. BREGGIN: Psychiatrist, went to Harvard College. Some of my training was at the Harvard Psychiatric Residency Program, then I spent two years after I finished my full psychiatric training at the National Institute of Mental Health. I've published about 20 books now, Michael—about 10 since you've known me—and about 30 to 40 scientific articles.

SAVAGE: You're one of my heroes because you dare speak out against the guilds that are so awfully powerful. Recently the so-called American Academy of Pediatrics had the audacity to come out and say that children as young as two years of age should be given adult anti-cholesterol drugs, without having done a single scientific study on the possible negative effects of such drugs on a child's liver, muscles, etc. You know and I know that it's because they were paid by the drug companies to do this, whether directly or indirectly through grants. Would you agree with the statement I just made?

DR. BREGGIN: Yes. What you find with the so-called experts in these areas is that if it has anything to do with drugs, you'll find that all of them—virtually all, Michael—are involved with the drug companies, getting research money. Some of them have paid professorships from the drug companies, or they're working in buildings on the medical school built by the drug companies. They might be doing seminars and consultations for the drug companies or publishing papers written by the drug companies. We've just had a scandal with a doctor at Harvard who worked more than any other person to try to justify drugging children in America. It turns out he's been hiding just how deep his connections are. In fact, I blew the whistle on him in my new book, *Medication Madness,* and now the whistling is even louder since the book was published a couple of weeks ago.

SAVAGE: Yeah, he should go to prison as far as I'm concerned. Anyone who treats children this way—or mistreats them, rather—under the guise of being their protector is a master of deceit who should be put in prison. You agree that true autism exists: correct or incorrect?

DR. BREGGIN: There's no doubt that there is a picture that develops in some children that causes them to have a terrible time relating to other human beings. It can be very lasting, especially if it isn't handled properly. And the way to handle it, which almost all of the genuine autism advocates talk about, is with psycho-social and educational means of nurturing and encouraging the child's capacity to learn and to relate to other kids. But, it's not proven to be biological.

SAVAGE: Isn't it true, by what I've read of Albert Einstein, that when he was very young he was a silent child? He stared off into space; he wouldn't talk to the teacher. In fact, the teacher would yell at him. I read this, and—I don't know if it's corroborated—that they shook him to get him to talk because he was considered somewhat "off-base." By today's definition, wouldn't Einstein have been declared autistic?

DR. BREGGIN: He would have certainly been put in the spectrum disorder—not autistic, probably, but in the spectrum disorder. Absolutely. He was very slow. He was not socially very skilled. It was very noticeable when he was young.

SAVAGE: Is it true that they've developed pharmaceuticals that don't really work, to give to these poor children?

DR. BREGGIN: They have now approved the most deadly of all drugs in the psychiatric arsenal to give to autistic kids who are "very irritable."

SAVAGE: And what drug is that?

DR. BREGGIN: Risperdal, which is an anti-psychotic drug, developed on the basis of subduing state mental hospital patients—

SAVAGE: Oh my God, no!

DR. BREGGIN: Yes, the worst of the drugs, Michael, in my work. I do a lot of medical, legal work. I do a lot of consultations with injured patients. I've already seen—well, this happened in October of 2006, and even before that I had seen two or three dozen children with permanent neurological diseases caused by Risperdal. In particular, a disease called Tardive Dyskinesia, which causes deterioration in the motor control and, to some extent, the mental centers of the brain. This produces abnormal twitches, blinking, and spasms that can affect the way the child walks, stands, sits, and can cause deformation. You can just imagine what that does to a child socially.

These are very deadly drugs. In fact, the drug company, Eli Lilly, that makes a very similar drug, Zyprexa, has now settled for over a billion dollars for cases of diabetes caused by this type of drug. And yet, the National Institute of Mental Health, which should be the National Institute of Medical Child Abuse at this point in time, didn't used to be like this. When I was there for two years as a full-time consultant, it was not like this. They have a handout where they go against all sanity and autism research and correct treatment. Instead, they talk about using drugs like Risperdal for behavior problems in children!

SAVAGE: Now, if you go on Google and do a search on Risperdal, listen to the side ads: "Help for mood swings. Do you have bipolar?" And these are medical groups—hospitals, psychiatric groups—trying to invite people to come and be diagnosed bi-polar or whatever they want to be called. Is this not a business today, Dr. Breggin?

DR. BREGGIN: It's horrible. It's an unethical business. When I was in psychiatric training, my entire four-year period, post-medical school, three and one half of that were in psychiatry, I saw two or three manic patients, people totally out of control. Today that's what is called bipolar. Now, every doctor has 10 or 15 in his practice—or 20, if he has a big practice. And it's all, or almost all, being caused by the SSRI antidepressants, which commonly drive people into mania. So, it's a business that actually supports itself. First, you give the child Ritalin. Then the child can't sleep, so you give him a sedative. Then the child gets sad from the combination of drugs and you give him an antidepressant. And that drives him into mania, and you tell the parents he has bipolar disorder. So help me God, Michael—I see this again and again in my practice.

SAVAGE: I think you would agree that common sense has gone out of the American social community. Any last words?

DR. BREGGIN: I think that you *do* need to be defended. You are pointing out a crisis in America with the diagnosing and drugging of our children. I wish the people who were attacking you would, instead, defend their children from psychiatric child abuse. That's what I believe, in essence, you are trying to say.

SAVAGE: Dr. Breggin, you're one of my heroes. You have been for years.

After I interviewed Dr. Breggin, I received calls from several individuals, who had interesting things to say about my commentary regarding autism. Their personal experiences support my claims on many different levels.

School Psychologist:

KYLE: I have been working with children with autism for the past 10 years. I'm currently a school psychologist and wanted to point out to the listeners that, you know, it's not just the medical field, but also the field of education. There're a lot of people who misclassify autism at that level. It's something that happens all the time.

SAVAGE: You're a school psychologist. You've worked in it for 10 years. If a child is diagnosed as autistic, what benefits befall the family? Let me ask you as a layman: does the child get additional tutoring help for free? Does the child get the ability to take tests outside of the normal classroom? Does the child get any other benefits in any way?

KYLE: Yes: State by state it varies. Some children will qualify for a certain level of speech services; they may get 10 hours or five hours of speech, depending on their classification. It's important to point out that—I know we're talking about autism, but even with the field of learning disabilities, children are misdiagnosed constantly. It's a very sad fact that exists in our society today that—and what people need to understand is—the people who suffer from this misdiagnosis are the children who really have the disorder.

SAVAGE: Well, we agree on that, and the money and treatment and therapy should be reserved for them, not for the falsely or misdiagnosed or the others who are put in the category for the benefits.

KYLE: I know many people might have been offended when they heard your comments taken out of context. But the truth of the matter is, this is a serious issue that somebody needs to bring attention to, because if somebody doesn't, there are a lot of people out there that have—you know—that are just in it for the money and not to help children. That's the problem.

SAVAGE: Look, Kyle, you're a school psychologist. You've worked in the field for 10 years. When you said, "They're in it for the money," let's go down to that level. What do you mean "in it for the money"? What money is involved?

KYLE: Well, there's a lot of money involved. Take, for example, the screeners that are highly acknowledged. The publishing companies make a lot of money off these screeners. The interventions that are put out there, that aren't empirically supported (meaning there's no research behind it)—a lot of that, people are making a lot of money from. I work with families who, no exaggeration, have spent tens of thousands of dollars on treatments that are completely invalid.

The hardest part of my job is to explain to these parents that there is no research behind it. I have to point these families in the right direction, but it's a very difficult thing to accomplish because the media and the Internet portray things in a very inaccurate fashion.

SAVAGE: Kyle, you are amazing in the sense that you are a school psychologist, you work with autism, and yet, you're willing to speak out. But this doesn't diminish the actual pain and suffering of a child with autism, does it?

KYLE: That's right, and the suffering that their families go through.

SAVAGE: But that's exactly my point.

Parent of Autistic Child:

SUSAN: I actually have two boys that were late in talking. It wasn't until last year when my three year old was diagnosed with ASD (Autism Spectrum Disorder), even though he scored in a non-autistic range, that they urged me to sign that he had some sort of autism so he could get services. They pretty much were bullying me to do it.

SAVAGE: Now when you say "they" bullied you to sign that he had this illness to get services, whom are you referring to, please?

SUSAN: My diagnosis did not come from the medical community. It came from the school district.

SAVAGE: Aha. Okay, it was the school district who was encouraging you to say, "Yes, sign on the dotted line: 'My child has autism'"?

SUSAN: Absolutely.

SAVAGE: Why would they want that, do you suppose?

SUSAN: I don't know. They were trying to push me into putting him into a special-education class five days a week.

SAVAGE: I see. So they have special-ed for children who are diagnosed in these categories—that's very interesting unto itself. Of course, we all know that special-ed and other such services are quite expensive. They may be bankrupting our schools. Yet, I have to emphasize: there is true autism, and those children are suffering, and they deserve the care that they are entitled to.

Therapist:

TIKVAH: I'm an ABA (Applied Behavioral Analysis) therapist with a prominent agency in New York. Today the agencies have really co-opted that term "autism." What they do is send the parents to neurologists that are willing to give this diagnosis to children that I have been working with—and I know for a fact that they're not autistic. They're mentally retarded, they're neurologically impaired, they have severe brain damage. They're labeled "autistic" because the agencies make more money with this label.

SAVAGE: You mean there's more money if the child's declared to be autistic rather than brain damaged?

TIKVAH: The state pays much more money for a child that's labeled "autistic" for ABA therapy than they would otherwise.

SAVAGE: No wonder I've touched a raw nerve.

We're talking about autism here: about whether too many children are being categorized as autistic; about my comments, which are often taken out of context. My comments about autism were aimed at the children who are falsely or misdiagnosed, and they were meant to boldly awaken parents to the medical community's attempt to label far too many children or adults as autistic. I stick to that. I will say it again: I know firsthand what it is like to have a child who suffers in front of your eyes.

My book *Healing Children Naturally* was first published in 1982. I re-published it in 2007. It's interesting that there is no reference to autism in this book. I have virtually every other childhood illness that was known at the time, including hyperactivity syndrome, but there's no reference to autism in my book. That is because it was little known, little understood, and hardly a problem at that time.

But I want to show you one paragraph: if you look up hyperactivity on page 217 from *Healing Children Naturally:* "If Tom Sawyer were alive today and in grade school, no doubt he would be declared a hyperactive child by a teacher eager to subdue him. To apply a medical term to social behavior is the road to *1984* and all the implied dangers of mind control and psychoactive drugs. I have long felt that the teachers who recommend Ritalin and other forms of speed-like drugs to control our children ought to be threatened with legal action from parents on the premise that teachers are not licensed to practice medicine and make diagnoses."

There's a preface in the book that opens with a one-liner: "Just as the undrawn sword is the mark of the best swordsman, so too is the best physician who relies least on synthetic drugs to heal."

I want to reiterate a few points: doctors in the United Kingdom National Screening Committee do not screen for autism in the general child population. Why? Because they say screening tools have not been fully validated. And interventions—that is, treatments—lack sufficient evidence for effectiveness. So, be careful.

We know that autism, by itself in a true case, is devastating. Its causes are unknown; we don't know what the cure is. Professor Steven Camarata of Vanderbilt University is quoted on my show as saying, "Because there are no reliable biomedical markers for autism, diagnosis must rely on subjective rating scales, making it difficult, if not impossible, to conduct accurate screening in toddlers or preschoolers." And yet, the medical quacks have said that there should be a diagnosis of every child down to 18 months! Well, let me repeat: The UK "recommends against screening for autism in the general child population because screening tools have not been fully validated and interventions lack sufficient evidence for effectiveness."

Now, let me read you some of the diagnostic categories for autism: "Lining objects up" makes a child autistic? Are you aware of the fact that there is a category now called the Autistic Spectrum? Are you aware that they have changed the definition of autism, and that is why they now say that up to 1 out of 160 children are autistic? What is the Autistic Spectrum? Well, what if your child has a very high IQ? What if your child is simply late in talking? Well, they might be placed into the Autistic Spectrum and invited to be treated.

Now, what do you mean by the "Autistic Spectrum"? Well, what if you wore glasses. Should you be included in the "blindness spectrum"? What if you had moles on your face? Should your moles place you on the "cancer spectrum"? Autism is very serious. Blindness and cancer are very serious—but to use definitions that make the situation impossible to be accurately diagnosed is an insult to the truly ill. So, these loose definitions of autism are the problem.

Another parent speaks out:

VIRGINIA: I'm the parent of an autistic son. There are quite a few things that I agree with you on. One: my son is 14 now. Trying to get him diagnosed with autism 12 years ago was like jumping through hoops. Today, you can go and in two visits, boom. Your child is autistic. I heard you talk about the broad spectrum of autism. Back then you had to prove many things just to get him diagnosed. My son is autistic, he has Asperger syndrome, and he also has Tourettes.

Nowadays, people push and—what I hear from his teachers—they push to get these kids in because they don't want to handle their brat-like behavior. They don't want to have to deal with, "Oh, my son is so spoiled rotten he throws a temper tantrum every time he doesn't get what he wants." The first thing they do is throw them on Ritalin.

SAVAGE: There you go. And you're a parent of an autistic child, and you actually have heard what I have said and what I'm saying: that the scarce resources should be preserved and reserved for people like yourself with a really ill child, as opposed to the fakers who are put in there either because they want the benefits, or because they're lazy, or they're misdiagnosed. That's the whole point. I'm so glad we're having this discussion because—I'm going to tell you right now, Victoria—no matter what people think of me, they're going to thank me. In the long run, I'm going to be thanked for having opened up a national dialogue on this phenomenally broad spectrum called autism that has been developed by the guilds of professionals who are making a fortune off the poor children.

What is ironic is that I, Michael Savage, who has personally devoted most of my life to the defense of defenseless children—to helping children stay off drugs, to helping parents understand that there's a very evil empire of pharmaceutical firms and corrupt doctors who wish to drug your children—I raised the issue of autism. The issue of autism came up because, in the context of talking about welfare fraud on my radio show, I began talking about fraudulent diagnoses in order to sell children medications.

I don't know if you folks out there understand that they're now claiming that 1 out of 160 children are autistic. This is statistically improbable. My radio comments about autism were meant to boldly awaken parents and children to the medical community's attempt to label far too many children or adults as autistic. Just as some drug companies have over-diagnosed ADD and ADHD to peddle dangerous speed-like drugs to children as young as four years of age, this cartel of doctors and drug companies is now creating a national panic by over-diagnosing autism, a disorder for which there is no definitive medical diagnosis.

Let me reiterate that there is no definitive medical diagnosis for autism—none! There are no blood chemistry changes, no MRI changes. There is no definitive medical diagnosis; it is all subjective. Did you know that if your child lines up his shoes under his bed, as I did as a child, your 'educator' might say he's autistic and throw him into the category of autism? If your child puts things on top of each other, as I did as a child, he's autistic? This is total insanity.

Be very mindful of the fact that there are fortunes being made in the medical and educational communities. Now, having said that, I'll repeat what I said before: the real cases of autism deserve our sympathy and our financial support. It is the phonies and the misdiagnosed and falsely diagnosed that I am addressing. Autism, in its true form, is a tragedy for the child and the parents, but to throw every child who evidences these characteristics into this category is a crime against the child.

I have a friend who called me and said that his son had a nervous tick at some point in his development. The pediatrician said, "Your child is autistic." My friend said, "That can't be. He just has a tick. He's a child, they outgrow it." The doctor said, "Oh no, he's autistic. We've got to treat him." The doctor was wrong; the friend was right. The friend never told his child he was autistic. Good that he didn't because the child outgrew the tick! I'm telling you, people: stop being led around by your nose by an industry that is filled with vultures.

Chapter Notes

Louie and His Monkey
"Monkeys Rampage in Indian Capital," *AFP*, November 12, 2007.

Islamists Are Winning
Belien, Paul. "Nazis and Islamists." The Brussels Journal Blog, November 11, 2007.

Separate Bedrooms
"U.S. Couples Seek Separate Bedrooms," *BBC News*, March 12, 2007.
http://news.bbc.co.uk/2/hi/americas/6441131.stm

Political Museums and the Downfall of American Culture
Martinfield, Sean. "Nan Kempner—American Chic." *The San Francisco Sentinel,* June 28, 2007.

New York Times Ad: Sex Doesn't Sell
La Ferla, Ruth. "Sex Doesn't Sell: Miss Prim Is In," *New York Times,* February 15, 2004, Style section.

Man Is a Creature of Reason
Buddha. *Teaching of Buddha.* Bukkyo Dendo Kyokai (BDK).

Thanks to Thomas Nelson Publishers for permission to reprint the following stories:

From *The Enemy Within* by Michael Savage, Nashville: Nelson Current, 2003. "Dead Man's Pants", pg. 7-8 and "Fat Pat & Tippy the Dog."

From *Liberalism is a Mental Disorder* by Michael Savage, Nashville: Nelson Current, 2005. "Sam the Butcher" and "White Men Need Not Apply."

From *The Savage Nation* by Michael Savage, Nashville: WND Books, 2002. "Fat Al's Tuna."